AD LIMINA

ADDRESSES

**The Addresses of
His Holiness Pope John Paul II
to the Bishops of the United States
during Their *Ad Limina* Visits**

MARCH 5–DECEMBER 9, 1988

ISBN 1-55586-271-3

Contents

Introduction

The *ad limina*, the periodic visit to Rome of every residential bishop to report on the state of his diocese, began in the fourth century of the Church's history. The bishops from the United States who made their *ad limina* (literally, to the threshold) visits in the Year of Our Lord 1988 found fresh evidence that these encounters with the See of Peter are much more than a bureaucratic formality. They are a visible expression of the unity of the bishops with Peter's successor. They provide a vehicle through which the Bishop of Rome can obtain reliable information on the state of the various churches throughout the world. Equally important, they are a vital instrument for pope and bishops to collaborate on their mutual concern for the care of the Church and the increasing efficacy of its methods for evangelization.

There is universal agreement that Pope John Paul II has given a renewed stimulus to the *ad limina* visits, demonstrating an intense personal interest in discussing pastoral problems and providing the bishops with encouragement and guidance in doctrinal and pastoral discourses of the kind contained in this book. The pope gave these addresses to groups of bishops who traveled from the United States between March and December of 1988. Richly intellectual, deeply theological, highly personalist, insightful and probing, warm and supportive—they are clearly the work of John Paul II. They do not exist in a vacuum. The pope has spoken often of how much he learned about the Church in this country in his 1979 and 1987 pastoral visits. These talks provide a convincing demonstration of the depth of his knowledge of the strengths and challenges of the Church in America.

Thus, for example, he speaks with admiration of the network of institutions and programs supported by the Church in this country for the relief of human suffering and need. He pays tribute to Catholic Relief Services as a dramatic example of solidarity with the needy. He cites approvingly the bishops' pastoral letters on peace and on economic justice and notes that "as pastors of the Church you are daily experiencing, especially in the case of migrants and immigrants, the tragic and pressing problems of poverty." He strongly praises the bishops' efforts to oppose abortion and defend human

1

life from conception onward, for example, through the annual "Respect Life Program."

Discussing the Church's magisterium, Pope John Paul II commends "unity with diversity" and the "necessary climate of freedom in the Church"; he recognizes a legitimate pluralism in theology. He also points out that the extent of such pluralism is intrinsically limited by "the unity of faith and the teachings of the Church's authentic magisterium." He deplores the deleterious effect that the so-called right to dissent has had upon Catholics—from whatever part of the spectrum—who give only selective adherence to the Church's moral doctrine.

Noting that the eucharist and the sacramental mystery of the Church are intimately linked to evangelization, the pope declares that "only with these means will the Church be herself and have the strength to fulfill her mission." He therefore applauds the tradition of eucharistic participation by the Catholics of the United States. "The time is ripe," he says, "to renew gratitude to God for this great gift and to reinforce this splendid tradition." To the crisis of the sacrament of penance, the pope gives particular attention, declaring the sacrament to be a matter of "supreme importance for the conversion and reconciliation of the world."

There is much more that the pope said in the *ad limina* talks, and it is all contained in the pages that follow. Those who would know the agenda of the Church in the United States for decades to come do well to read and ponder their contents.

William Ryan
Deputy Director
Office for Media Relations
Department of Communications
United States Catholic Conference

First Address of His Holiness
Pope John Paul II
to the Bishops of the United States
during Their *Ad Limina* Visits

March 5, 1988

Dear Brothers in our Lord Jesus Christ,

1. With this visit there begins the 1988 series of the *ad limina* visits of the American bishops. Today, I am very pleased to welcome all of you who make up the first group and who come from the ecclesiastical provinces of Dubuque, Kansas City, Omaha, and St. Louis. You represent a great cross section of the Catholic people of the United States, bringing with you, as you do, the hopes and aspirations, the joys and difficulties of so many people—individuals, families, and entire particular churches within the states of Iowa, Kansas, Nebraska, and Missouri.

For all of us, this is an hour of ecclesial communion that follows closely upon my second visit to the United States and especially our important meeting in Los Angeles. There is, moreover, a continuity between this present series of *ad limina* visits and that of 1983, which in turn was in continuity with my first visit to America in 1979. All of these encounters are likewise linked to the future of the Church in the United States, which I hope to be able to reflect on again next year in a meeting with American bishops.

2. Because this present hour is one of ecclesial communion, it is linked to our own salvation. The Church began her Lenten celebration proclaiming with St. Paul: "Now is the acceptable time! Now is the day of salvation!" (2 Cor 6:2). Like all the other members of the Church, we ourselves must approach our salvation in faith—faith in the mystery of Jesus Christ and his Church. As bishops, we put this faith into practice by actuating the mystery of our own hierarchical communion in the Church. By living this mystery of communion today, we are giving the response of faith to Christ as he holds up before us his design of unity for his Church and for all who make up the college of bishops.

On this occasion, you and I, united in ecclesial communion as pastors of individual dioceses in America and as the pastor of the universal Church respectively, have the task of offering to Jesus Christ, the supreme Shepherd of the entire flock, the Church in the United States. This Church belongs to Jesus Christ by right. He loves her intensely and intends to possess her ever more fully and to purify her ever more deeply in every aspect of her ecclesial reality.

3. I wish to express, once again, sentiments of profound gratitude and satisfaction at having been able to visit for a second time the Church in the United States and to have experienced so many aspects of her life. Coupled with these sentiments are also those of admiration for everything that the grace of Christ has accomplished in the lives of God's people in your land. The ecclesial reality in the United States is an expression of the power of Christ's paschal mystery at work in the lives of countless individuals and numerous communities. Over and over again this ecclesial reality deserves our prayerful reflection.

During the course of my September visit to nine dioceses, I was able to experience the life of faith that is lived in all 186 dioceses throughout the United States, which include 12 Eastern-rite dioceses and the military ordinariate. What was especially gratifying was to meet all the various categories that make up the one people of God: bishops, priests, deacons, religious, seminarians, and religious in formation, and the Catholic laity. All of these categories were present not only in special encounters arranged for me but in the large liturgical celebrations held in each diocese. Repeatedly, I witnessed the faith of a Church that could address herself to God in the words of the psalm: "I will give you thanks in the vast assembly; in the mighty throng I will praise you" (Ps 35:18). And again: "I will give thanks to the Lord with all my heart in the company and assembly of the just. Great are the works of the Lord, exquisite in all their delights" (Ps 111:1-2).

In every event in which I took part, the local bishop was at my side. Together, we experienced the Church as she is incarnate in the historical, geographical, social, economic, political, and religious context of the United States of America. I saw. I listened. I was addressed. I spoke. And the Church prayed—Christ prayed in his Body, in us, the Church. And all of us entered into closer communion with each other and with him, the supreme Shepherd.

4. My particular role throughout the whole visit was to proclaim Jesus Christ as the Son of God and the redeemer of man—every man, woman, and child. At the same time, I came to America in

order to ask everyone to meet Jesus Christ and to give him the response of faith: to believe in his name, to accept his word, to be open to his love and the love of his Father and the Holy Spirit.

At the basis of all my exhortations to fraternal solidarity and love was that pivotal truth proclaimed by the Second Vatican Council: "By his incarnation the Son of God united himself in a certain way with each human being" (*Gaudium et Spes*, 22). The Incarnation as the expression of God's love is the new foundation of human dignity for everyone. Hence, I could not speak of God's love without speaking of human dignity and what it requires. And so at the very beginning of my visit in Miami I stated: "I come to proclaim the Gospel of Jesus Christ to all who freely choose to listen to me; to tell again the story of God's love in the world; to spell out once more the message of human dignity with its inalienable human rights and its inevitable human duties" (September 10, 1987).

5. All of us were, in fact, able to perceive a great response of faith in so many ways on the part of the people—everything being accomplished by the Lord, in accordance with the words of the psalm: "Come! Behold the deeds of the Lord, the astounding things he has wrought" (Ps 46:9). This response of faith was evident in the wonderful collaboration and hard work of preparation for my visit, in the understanding and acceptance of my role as the successor of the apostle Peter, in an openness to the proclamation of the gospel message, and in our common worship. In so many ways, the people expressed their faith in the Church as she exists by the will of Christ: both particular and universal.

One of the great riches of the Church in the United States is the way in which she herself incarnates universality or catholicity in her ethnic makeup, taken as she is "from every nation and race, people and tongue" (Rv 7:9). The Church in the United States has the advantage of being naturally disposed to live catholicity and to show solidarity with all those particular churches where her people came from originally. The ethnic contributions to the various liturgies celebrated during my visit were not mere folkloric expressions; they were rather keys opening the door to a fuller understanding of the ecclesial reality of the Church in the United States.

In witnessing aspect after aspect of the Church in your land, I was conscious in each diocese of the mystery of the universal Church as she subsists in particular churches that joyfully make their pilgrimage of faith, amid obstacles and opposition, to the Father of our Lord Jesus Christ.

The ecclesial reality presented to me in each diocesan community was a portion of Christ's flock, invested with his Spirit—as poured out through the paschal mystery—and living by the same Spirit. It was the Church of Christ living the mystery of redemption in the modern world, being herself continually purified after her immersion into the bath of regeneration (cf. Eph 5:26).

6. As the Church in the United States works to be faithful to her task of actuating the kingdom of God in its initial stage, she strives earnestly to meet pastoral challenges all around her, the fundamental one of which is to be constantly converted or renewed in God's love. Being convinced of the openness of the Church in the United States to challenge, of her good will and, above all, of Christ's grace active within her, I too challenged her in various ways, including setting before her the need to be open to renewal by God himself.

In effect, being renewed in God's love has very concrete requirements for the whole Church and, hence, for the Church in the United States. It means that she must live to the full her vocation to holiness. In the world, she must be herself; she must always be what she is meant to be: the holy Body of Christ. In chapter 5 of *Lumen Gentium*, the Church has given to all her sons and daughters a great gift in clearly enunciating the universal call to holiness: "All Christ's followers therefore are invited and bound to pursue holiness and the perfect fulfillment of their proper state" (42). The application of this principle to married couples, Christian parents, widowed and single people is of extreme importance. The Church is truly the sacrament of holiness for everyone. The council insisted "that all the faithful of Christ of whatever rank or status are called to the fullness of Christian life and to the perfection of charity" (ibid., 40).

How important it was for the whole Church that the council should so strongly present this challenge to the laity! Without this principle, the full participation of the laity in the life and mission of the Church could never have been ensured. The universal call to holiness was also at the basis of the recent Synod of Bishops on the laity.

Specific consequences of this principle have been spelled out in the pastoral constitution *Gaudium et Spes*, which does not admit "false opposition between professional and social activities on the one part, and religious life on the other" and which tells us that the "split between the faith which many profess and their daily lives deserves to be counted among the more serious errors of our age" (43).

7. As the Church in all her own members endeavors to live her vocation of holiness, she is also mindful of her obligation to help all people to discover in Christ's redemption the full meaning of life in this world. This is another great challenge for the Church. At the beginning of my pontificate I expressed it in my first encyclical, saying: "The Church's fundamental action in every age and particularly in ours is to direct man's gaze, to point the awareness and experience of the whole of humanity toward the mystery of Christ, to help all people to be familiar with the profundity of the redemption taking place in Christ Jesus" (*Redemptor Hominis*, 10).

This challenge to help all people to be open to the redemption is linked with the Church's missionary activity and therefore with her own missionary nature. The Church in the United States—like the universal Church—must be committed to this cause today and forever. During my visit to Phoenix, I had the opportunity to touch upon this vital aspect of the Church's life, citing also the American bishops' 1986 pastoral statement on world mission. The question that I asked in Phoenix still requires further answers from the Church both in the United States and throughout the world: "Who will respond to God's missionary call at the end of the 20th century?"

8. To bring the fullness of God's word to people, to point their gaze to the mystery of Christ, to help them to understand human dignity and the meaning of life through the key of the redemption is the supreme service of the Church to humanity. The Church renders this service in the name of Christ and through the power of his Spirit. At the same time, she knows that in consequence of the principle of the Incarnation—Christ's union with every human being—she must constantly link with her missionary activity and all her work of evangelization a vast program to help meet other human needs. She is vitally interested in making her specific contribution to uplifting humanity to the level that corresponds to the rightful dignity already granted to it in the mystery of the Word made flesh.

The Church finds in Jesus Christ, the Incarnate Word, the principle of her solicitude for humanity, for the future of humanity on earth and for the whole of development and progress (cf. *Redemptor Hominis*, 15). All of the Church's motives are inspired by the Gospel of Christ (cf. *Sollicitudo Rei Socialis*, 47).

The mission of solidarity, to which I have dedicated my latest encyclical and on which there will be further opportunities for reflection, represents a specially grave responsibility for the Church today. During my visit to the United States, I was able to see with what seriousness the local churches have responded to the needs of their brothers and sisters, with what generosity they have striven to alleviate suffering and pain, with what alacrity they have shown their solidarity with humanity. Not only do I recall the panorama of charitable works and health care that was presented to me in San Antonio and Phoenix, and also efforts of many of your local churches to respond to the farm crisis, but I know the commitment of all the people of God in America to carry out their vocation of Christian service.

This challenge of service, with its motivation in Christ and his Gospel, must accompany the Church in the United States during the whole length of her pilgrimage of faith. Acceptance of this challenge is extremely pleasing to God; failure to do so is fatal. The Second Vatican Council reminds us, "The Christian who neglects his temporal duties neglects his duties toward his neighbor and even God and jeopardizes his eternal salvation" (*Gaudium et Spes*, 43).

These and other challenges, dear brothers, stand before the Church of God and the United States—a beloved Church living in the power of Christ's Spirit and called to ever greater holiness of life, especially during this Marian Year of grace. As you rise up humbly with your people to meet these challenges, you have every reason to be filled with hope. In all your efforts to live worthily the mystery of the Church, you are supported by the prayers of the Blessed Virgin Mary, who "as a sign of sure hope and solace" (*Lumen Gentium*, 68) accompanies you on your pilgrimage of faith toward the final goal of eternal life in Christ Jesus. As you make your pilgrim way along this path, I ask you to take deep encouragement from the words of the prophet: "The Lord God is in your midst, a mighty savior; he will rejoice over you with gladness and renew you in his love" (Zep 3:17).

In this love, I send my apostolic blessing to all your local churches, being especially mindful of all those who bear the cross of Christ in pain and suffering.

Second Address of His Holiness
Pope John Paul II
to the Bishops of the United States
during Their *Ad Limina* Visits

April 16, 1988

Dear Brothers in our Lord Jesus Christ,

1. It is a great pleasure for me to welcome all of you, the bishops of Texas, Oklahoma, and Arkansas. In you, I greet all your beloved faithful and each of your local churches with all its priests, deacons, religious, seminarians, and laity. I recall with special joy my recent visit to San Antonio, the wonderful welcome given me, and the impressive faith of the people. I assure you that I remain close to you in your ministry of faith, as does the mother of Jesus, *La Virgen de Guadalupe*.

In my recent talk to your brother bishops of Region IX, I mentioned a series of related pastoral events that are, in effect, inspired by a single vision of faith and directed to the goals of deep personal renewal and ever more effective evangelical service in the United States. These events include the present *ad limina* visits and those of 1983, the papal visits of 1979 and 1987, as well as the meeting with American bishops foreseen for 1989.

Today, I would like to review in this context still another event— one which concerns the universal Church and therefore the Church in the United States. It is the great Jubilee of the Year 2000, marking the close of the second millennium of Christianity and the inauguration of the third. This anniversary requires of the whole Church a period of serious preparation at both the universal and local levels. From the beginning of my pontificate, and in particular in the encyclical *Redemptor Hominis,* I have attempted to direct the attention of the Church to the season of "a new Advent" (1), which precedes all the grace-filled opportunities and activities that we ardently hope for in the year 2000.

2. The aim of the jubilee and of its preparation is to "recall and reawaken in us in a special way our awareness of the key truth of

faith, which St. John expressed at the beginning of his Gospel: 'The Word became flesh and dwelt among us' (Jn 1:14)" (ibid.). The whole celebration of the millennium is meaningful only in the light of the mystery of the Incarnation and of its divine motivation and purpose, which are also explained to us by St. John when he says: "God so loved the world that he gave his only Son, that whoever believes in him may not die but may have eternal life" (Jn 3:16). Emphasizing these truths, the Church strives to provide a framework of principles from which she will continue to draw out from her life "the new and the old" (Mt 13:52) in order to elicit the response of faith to the Father's love and to his Incarnate Word, and to lead us all to eternal life.

By reflecting on the Incarnation, the Church of the year 2000 will be able to understand herself ever more fully in her twofold nature, human and divine. She will also understand the sublime union of these two elements in the everyday reality of her life as the body of the Word made flesh. The Church is convinced that, by placing the Incarnation before the people of God with all the power of her being, mankind will rediscover in this mystery of God's revealed love the truth that explains and directs all human activity. Only in the light of the Incarnation does all human living take on its proper perspective, or as I stated in that first encyclical: "Through the Incarnation God gave human life the dimension that he intended man to have from his first beginning" (1).

3. Our present pastoral efforts as bishops, those envisioned for 1989, and those beyond should be directed to creating that profound and dynamic vision that must characterize the Church in the year 2000. The Church of the millennium must have an increased consciousness of being the kingdom of God in its initial stage. She must show that she is vitally concerned with being faithful to Christ; hence, she must strive mightily to respond to the great challenges of holiness, evangelization, and service. At the same time, the Church of the millennium must emerge as a clear sign of her own eschatological state, living by faith the mystery that is yet to be fully revealed. As she does this, the Church must proclaim with St. Paul that "eye has not seen nor has ear heard what God has prepared for those who love him" (1 Cor 2:9).

The Church of the millennium will still be the Church undergoing purification through suffering—the salvific value of which she fully knows. Yet, in her purifying experience, the Church will still be able to cry out that the sufferings of this time are "as nothing compared with the glory to be revealed in us" (Rom 8:18). As a

Church living in expectation of glory to be revealed, she will find ever greater strength to proclaim the value of celibacy that is lived for the kingdom of God, the final state of which is in preparation: "Thy kingdom come!"

At such an important juncture of her life, the Church of the millennium must declare that she is ready at any moment to meet the Lord, just as she is ready to go on faithfully in joyful hope awaiting his coming. But in both her waiting and her expectation, she is reinforced in hope because she knows that Christ her head has gone before her in his ascension to prepare a place for her. And as she waits, she remembers what he once said to the disciples: "If I go and prepare a place for you, I will come back again and take you to myself, so that where I am you also may be" (Jn 14:3).

The Church is convinced of her right to be with Jesus, who, seated at the right hand of the Father, has already united her to himself in glory. The triumph of the head already belongs to the members of the body. This makes it easy for the Church as she lives the new Advent to accept with keen conviction the words of her victorious redeemer: "Remember, I am coming soon" (Rv 22:12). During the millennium, the Church is called upon to remember. It is also the special hour for the Church to respond with fidelity and confidence proclaiming by her actions and by her whole life: "Come Lord Jesus!" (v. 20).

4. The Church's program for the millennium and its preparation must be a total concentration on Jesus Christ. She must proclaim Jesus Christ as victorious in the redemption that he brought about in his blood; she must proclaim Jesus Christ, crucified and glorified, the one wearing "a cloak dipped in blood" and bearing the name "the Word of God" (Rv 19:13). The Church is called upon to proclaim the supreme effectiveness of Christ's death; to proclaim that the triumph of the lamb is already operative in the Church for two millennia, and that it belongs to all his chosen and faithful followers (cf. Rv 17:14). The Church's proclamation in the millennium must be the proclamation of her own victory over sin and death accomplished by him who is "the firstborn from the dead" (Rv 1:5) and who communicates this victory to all his members throughout the ages.

The Christ of the millennium is this firstborn from the dead, "the king of kings and lord of lords" (Rv 19:16), the eternal Son of God, the Word of God made flesh, the person who identifies himself as "the one who lives" (Rv 1:18) and who tells his Church: "There is nothing to fear!" (v. 17). It is precisely this Christ, divine and incarnate, that the Church presents to the world as the supreme exemplar of all human life. In this sense, the Church makes her own the presentation of Pontius Pilate: *"Ecco homo"* (Jn 19:5). The proclamation of the millennium will be the proclamation of this man Jesus Christ and in him the exaltation of all humanity. The Word, who remains forever with his Father and as such is the truth and life of humanity, in taking human flesh becomes the way for humanity (cf. St. Augustine, tract. *In Ioannem* 34,9).

The Christ of the millennium is the divine Christ of the Gospels who has entered into his glory and who is forever alive in his word and in his Church. He is not a weak and ineffective Christ but a Christ who has triumphed throughout twenty centuries and who remains "the power of God and the wisdom of God" (1 Cor 1:24). To those who accept him, moreover, he gives the power to become the children of God, to become by adoption what he is by nature— the Son of God. The Christ of the millennium is the man who has entered into the history of nations, has uplifted cultures by his message, transformed the destinies of peoples and who, in reveal-ing God to man, has revealed all humanity to itself (cf. *Gaudium et Spes*, 22).

5. The millennium becomes, therefore, the hour of our Christian identity in all its catholic universality. In order to celebrate the millennium effectively, the Church must recall her origin and reflect deeply on her mission. To do this, she must retrace the path she has taken up till now, bearing her apostolic message down the centuries, beginning "in Jerusalem, throughout Judea and Samaria, yes, even to the ends of the earth" (Acts 1:8). It is truly the appro-priate hour to foster a consciousness of Christian tradition and culture. These elements have found expression in the art, architec-ture, music, literature, and other expressions of genius that each generation and all generations together in the Church have created throughout the centuries in the name of Christ. There are many ways to foster this consciousness but certainly the means of social communications at our disposal must be utilized to the full.

6. Living in the Spirit sent to her by Christ, the Church looks forward to the millennium as a time of vast internal renewal. By his power, the Holy Spirit is truly able to effect in the Church a new Pentecost. On the part of all of us, however, this requires new attitudes of humility, generosity, and openness to the purifying action of the Spirit.

The whole concept of renewal must be seen in its relationship to penance and the eucharist. In *Redemptor Hominis*, I emphasized "that the Church of the new Advent . . . must be the Church of the eucharist and of penance" (20). Only with these means will the Church be herself and have the strength to fulfill her mission. The millennium is the supreme moment for the glorification of the cross of Christ and for the proclamation of forgiveness through his blood. I ask all the bishops of the Church—and today in a special way the bishops of the United States—to do everything possible in preparing for the millennium to promote the faithful observance of the centuries-old practice of individual confession, guaranteeing thereby the individual's right to a personal encounter with the crucified and merciful Christ, and the right of Christ to meet each one of us in the key moment of conversion and pardon (cf. ibid.).

Presiding over every celebration of the millennium will be the eucharistic Lord, himself renewing his Church and presenting her to the Father in union with himself. It is mainly through the eucharist that the millennium will actuate the power of the redemption. In the eucharist, the Church will find the sure source and guarantee of her commitment to the service of humanity.

From the eucharist, the Catholic laity will derive the strength to perform with joy and perseverance their specific role in the Church and in the world. During the millennium, there must be an ever more generous actuation of everything that the postsynodal document on the laity will propose for the life and mission of the laity.

7. In all her activities, the Church of the millennium must be totally absorbed with the task of bringing Christ to the world. This will require her to understand the world ever more deeply and to dialogue ever more intensely with all people of good will. As the Church does this with love and respect, and as she reinforces her own meekness—after the example of the meek and humble Christ— she must at the same time shed any remnant of fear at the prospect of displeasing the world when she presents to it her founder's message in all its purity and with all its exigencies. She must also divest herself of any trace of defensiveness as she acknowledges Christ to be forever "a sign of contradiction," and proclaims his teaching on issues such as truth, justice, evangelical peacemaking, and chastity.

The pastoral statement of the bishops of Texas on human sexuality represents a much appreciated pastoral effort to present the Church's teaching on chastity without fear or reticence, with trust in the power of truth and the grace of God.

The whole event of the millennium is the hour for the apostolic Church to bear witness to the Christ who sent her to the nations, telling her: "Teach them to carry out everything I have commanded you, and know that I am with you always" (Mt 28:20).

8. Dear Brothers: What I wish to do today is leave with you and with the whole Church in America a vision of the millennium as a pastoral initiative, an ecclesial event, a response of faith to the God who "so loved the world that he gave his only Son" (Jn 3:16). This vision must be captured by the whole Church in the United States and expressed in each diocese, each parish, each community. All the institutions in the Church must be challenged by this spiritual event. The Church's fidelity to Christ is at stake in the way she will proclaim the Incarnation and the redemption, in the way she will celebrate, interiorly and publicly, the most important anniversary that humanity has ever known.

Whereas the year 2000 still seems somewhat distant, the period of "the new Advent" is already a reality for the Church. Long-range preparations are needed now. Theological reflections must help to reinforce the faith of God's people, so that they may mightily proclaim their Redeemer by word and deed in the great jubilee. Your own pastoral zeal and creativity will help you to prepare worthily your local churches for this event and to adopt means commensurate with the goals to be attained. All the faithful of the Church must understand the spirit of the millennium so that they can all contribute to its preparation and celebration.

By their very nature, the seminaries in your country must fulfill a key role in the renewal required by the millennium. Together with their bishops, the priests of the new Advent must be able to unite their communities around the person of the Redeemer and to give spiritual leadership in bringing forth a new Christian humanism.

The special support of prayer and penance must be sought from contemplative religious and that of salvific suffering from all the sick. Catholic institutions of higher learning must contribute with faith by enunciating ever more clearly the gospel heritage in its relationship to all human learning. All the categories of God's people must be invited to unite in a great hymn of praise: "To him who loves us and frees us from our sins by his blood . . . to him be glory and power forever and ever" (Rv 1:5).

May this hymn of praise to the Redeemer, dear brothers, truly resound throughout Texas, Oklahoma, Arkansas, and the whole United States during the new Advent and in preparation for the jubilee celebration itself.

Third Address of His Holiness
Pope John Paul II
to the Bishops of the United States
during Their *Ad Limina* Visits

June 1, 1988

Dear Brothers in our Lord Jesus Christ,

1. Once again it is a great joy for me to welcome a group of American bishops. In you, I greet all the priests, deacons, religious, and laity of the provinces of Louisville, Mobile, and New Orleans. Memories of New Orleans encourage me to send special greetings to those groups that I met there: the youth of America, the apostles of Catholic education, the beloved black community throughout your land, and all those striving to meet the challenge of greatness in higher Catholic education. At the same time, I remember in my thoughts and cherish in my heart all the faithful of America, for whom we are striving to provide true pastoral service in the name of "the chief Shepherd of the flock" (1 Pt 5:4), our Lord and Savior Jesus Christ.

In all the pastoral events that I experience with you, the bishops of the United States—each event in continuity with the preceding ones—it is my intention to reflect with you on an organic pastoral view of our episcopal ministry. This organic view must take into account the perennial exigencies of the Gospel; it must also express the indisputable priorities of the life of the Church today, both in her universal needs and in the special requirements of the Church in the United States. At the same time, it must faithfully reflect the call of the Second Vatican Council to reform and renewal as reiterated by the Bishop of Rome and the worldwide episcopate in communion with him. This communion is especially evident in the different sessions of the Synod of Bishops, the conclusions of which are of special urgency for all pastoral planning in the Church.

2. One of the essential themes of the Gospel that has been emphasized by both the Second Vatican Council and the Synod of Bishops is the call to penance or conversion—and consequently to

reconciliation—incumbent on all members of the Church, and particularly relevant to our own lives and ministry as bishops. Conversion as proclaimed by Christ is a whole program of life and pastoral action. It is the basis for an organic view of pastoral ministry because it is linked to all the great aspects of God's revelation.

Conversion speaks to us about the need to acknowledge the primacy of God in the world and in our individual lives. It presupposes the reality of sin and the need to respond to God in and through Christ the Savior, who frees us from our sins. Christ's command of conversion imposes on us "the obedience of faith" (Rom 1:5) in all its implications.

Conversion becomes for us a synthesis of the Gospel, and repeated conversions throughout the ages reflect the unceasing action of the risen Christ on the life of the Church. Jesus himself introduces us to the meaning of penance or conversion when he says, "Repent and believe in the Gospel" (Mk 1:15). Conversion signifies an internal change of attitude and of approach to God and to the world. This is the way the Church has always understood this reality. The synod of 1983 described it as "the inmost change of heart under the influence of the word of God and in the perspective of the kingdom," and again as "a conversion that passes from the heart to deeds, and then to the Christian's whole life" (*Reconciliatio et Paenitentia*, 4).

3. Our conversion is understood as a response to the call of Jesus to embrace his Gospel and enter his kingdom. His call had been anticipated by the precursor of his kingdom, John the Baptist: "Repent, for the kingdom of heaven is at hand" (Mt 3:2). Jesus himself entrusted this call to his apostles and, through them, to us. On the day of Pentecost, it was taken up by Peter, who encouraged the people to proclaim Jesus Christ as Lord and Messiah, saying, "Repent and be baptized, every one of you in the name of Jesus Christ for the forgiveness of your sins; and you will receive the gift of the Holy Spirit" (Acts 2:38). The apostle Paul bore public testimony to the fact that he "preached the need to repent and turn to God, and to do works giving evidence of repentance" (Acts 26:20).

In imitating the apostles Peter and Paul, by striving to embrace the reality of conversion and by preaching it, we are in effect proclaiming the full content of the truth that Jesus revealed about repentance. In speaking of conversion or penance, we direct people's attention to God himself and to the need to live in conformity with the truth that God has expressed regarding human nature. To call to conversion means to proclaim God's dominion over all creation, especially over all humanity. It means extolling God's law and acknowledging all the practical effects of creation. In the act of conversion, the human person proclaims his or her dependence on God and acknowledges the need to obey God's law in order to live in freedom.

Conversion presupposes an acknowledgment of the reality of human rebellion against the majesty of God. In each person's heart, conversion signifies the vast superiority of grace over sin, so much so that "where sin increased, grace overflowed all the more" (Rom 5:20). Conversion is made possible and actually brought about in human hearts by the victory of Jesus in his paschal mystery. Every individual conversion is an expression of the divine plan whereby human beings must consent to God's salvific action. Hence, every conversion expresses the nobility of human effort and, at the same time, its total insufficiency. Every conversion proclaims the supremacy of grace.

4. By reflecting on Jesus' words to be converted, to repent, to open our hearts to life and grace, to renounce sin, we discover the relations between conversion and God's love, the relationship between conversion and God's power. As we reflect on the call of Jesus to do penance, we discover the new world of mercy, which is revealed in the cross. The cross of Jesus Christ is indeed, as I have stated before, "a radical revelation of mercy, or rather of the love that goes against what constitutes the very root of evil in the history of man: against sin and death. . . . The cross of Christ, in fact, makes us understand the deepest roots of evil" (*Dives in Misericordia*, 8).

Mercy, in turn, presumes conversion on the part of all of us, and the notion of conversion forces us to reflect on the truth which we must live. It often happens that when the Church speaks of the requirements of truth in relation to conversion and mercy, the world reacts negatively. But the Church cannot proclaim the reality of God's infinite mercy without pointing out how the acceptance of mercy requires an openness to God's law. It requires the personal observance of God's law as a response to his covenant or mercy. In demonstrating his fidelity to his fatherly love, God cannot contradict his own truth. Hence, true conversion, which consists in discovering God's mercy, includes repentance from whatever negates the truth of God expressed in human nature.

5. At the same time, conversion brings with it reconciliation. Reconciliation is the result of conversion. It is the gift of the heavenly Father given through Christ and in the Holy Spirit to those who

are converted. In the words of St. Paul: God "has reconciled us to himself through Christ and given us the ministry of reconciliation" (2 Cor 5:18).

Conversion remains the key to all reconciliation and to the Church's ministry of reconciliation. All individual and collective reconciliation springs from the conversion of hearts. The social fabric of the Church and the world will be reformed and renewed only when conversion is interior and personal. The needed reform of oppressive economic and political structures in the world cannot be effected without the conversion of hearts. The reconciliation of humanity at the level of individuals, communities, peoples, and blocs of nations presumes the conversion of individual hearts and must be based on truth. The synod on reconciliation and penance fully proclaimed this truth, showing how at the basis of all divisions there is personal sin, the ultimate essence and darkness of which is "disobedience to God" (*Reconciliatio et Paenitentia*, 14; cf. 16).

6. In being called to be a sign of reconciliation in the world, the Church is therefore called to be a sign of conversion from sin and of obedience to God's law. In her very nature, the Church is the great sacrament of reconciliation. To live this truth fully, she must at all times be both a reconciled and reconciling community that proclaims the divisive power of every personal sin but above all the reconciling and unifying power of Christ's paschal mystery, in which love is stronger than sin and death.

In fidelity to her mission, the Church must preach the existence of evil and sin. With great insight, the Synod of Bishops acknowledged with Pope Pius XII that "the sin of the century is the loss of the sense of sin" (cf. ibid., 18). In the postsynodal apostolic exhortation, I noted that the "restoration of a proper sense of sin is the first way of facing the grave spiritual crisis looming over man today" (ibid.). Already the early Church had reacted vigorously to the illusion of sinlessness on the part of some, as stated in the First Letter of St. John: "If we say we have no sin, we deceive ourselves and the truth is not in us" (1 Jn 1:8).

When we take to heart this statement, we open ourselves to the action of the Holy Spirit, who reveals to us our limitations and defects and "convicts" us of our sins of act and omission. At the same time, both as individuals and as communities in the Church, we know that we have not yet reached our goal; we do not yet fully live the Gospel; we have not yet perfectly applied the council. The more we have a sense of our limitations and personal sins, the more we will divest ourselves of any sentiments of neotriumphalism and take to heart all pertinent observations and suggestions about our life and ministry.

7. Humbled before God and reconciled with him and within herself, the Church is able to pursue with interior freedom her specific mission, which is "to evoke conversion and penance in man's heart and to offer him the gift of reconciliation" (*Reconciliatio et Paenitentia*, 23). This she does in different ways, particularly through catechesis and the sacraments entrusted to her by Christ. At this moment in the Church's life, in the United States and throughout the world, it is opportune to reflect on the sacrament of penance with a view to reinforcing, in communion with the whole Church, an organic pastoral approach to a matter of such supreme importance for the conversion and reconciliation of the world.

The general experience of the bishops participating at the synod and of many others throughout the Church in regard to the use of this sacrament was summarized in this way: "The sacrament of penance is in crisis. . . . For the sacrament of confession is indeed being undermined" (ibid., 28). These statements are neither negative expressions of pessimism nor causes for alarm; they are rather expressions of a pastoral realism that requires positive pastoral reflection, planning, and action. By the power of Christ's paschal mystery that is active within her, the Church is capable of responding to all the crises that she ever faces, including this one. But she must make sure that she acknowledges the crisis and that she adequately faces it with the supernatural means at her disposal.

8. In this crisis, which becomes a challenge to the Church's fidelity, the bishops have a particular responsibility, which they can meet with a unique effectiveness. In something as sacred as this sacrament, sporadic efforts are not enough to overcome the crisis. For this reason, I appeal today to you and, through you, to all the bishops of the United States for organic pastoral planning in each diocese to restore the sacrament of penance to its rightful place in the Church and to renew its use in full accordance with the intention of Christ.

A key point in this renewal process is "the obligation of pastors to facilitate for the faithful the practice of integral and individual confession of sins, which constitutes for them not only a duty but also an inviolable and inalienable right, besides being something needed for the soul" (ibid., 33). In this task, the bishops need the support and fraternal collaboration of all concerned. Of special importance are the concerted efforts of all the members of the conference of bishops in insisting that the *gravis necessitas* required for general absolution be truly understood in the sense explained in canon 961. In various regions of the world, the crisis facing the sacrament of penance is due in part to unwarranted interpretations of what constitutes the conditions of the *gravis necessitas* envisioned by the Church. The bishops, not only of the United States but of all countries, can make a great pastoral contribution to the true renewal of the sacrament of penance by their sustained efforts to do everything possible to promote the proper interpretation of canon 961. At stake is the whole question of the personal relationship that Christ wills to have with each penitent and which the Church must unceasingly defend. In the encyclical *Redemptor Hominis*, I spoke of this relationship as involving rights on the part of each individual and of Christ himself (cf. 20).

9. As bishops, we also contribute to true renewal by fraternally encouraging our priests to persevere in their incomparable ministry as confessors. This means that they must first travel this path of conversion and reconciliation themselves (cf. *Reconciliatio et Paenitentia*, 29). In this, too, we must give them an example. Priests are meant by Christ to find immense spiritual fulfillment in accomplishing the Church's "ministry of reconciliation" (2 Cor 5:11) in a unique and supremely effective manner.

Reflection of the sacrament of penance as the sacrament of conversion and reconciliation will truly help individuals and communities within the Church to understand the real nature of the renewal called for by the Second Vatican Council. The sacrament of penance is the actuation of Christ's pastoral victory because it is the personal application of his reconciling action to individual hearts. Without the proper use of the sacrament of penance, all other forms of renewal will be incomplete and, at the same time, the very reform and renewal of structure will be limited. For this reason, the sacrament of reconciliation will prove to be a true key to social progress and a sure measure of the authenticity of all renewal in the Church in the United States and throughout the world.

10. As we move closer toward the year 2000, we must ever more effectively proclaim the fullness of Christ's mercy and offer to the world the hope that is found only in a loving and forgiving Savior. In order to accomplish this, we are called to do everything possible to promote the sacrament of mercy and forgiveness in accordance with the Second Vatican Council, the pertinent liturgical norms of the Church, the *Code of Canon Law,* and the conclusions of the synod of 1983 as formulated in *Reconciliatio et Paenitentia.* A goal of this magnitude cannot be attained without the constantly renewed col-

legial commitment of the worldwide episcopate. Today, in particular, I ask this commitment of you and all your brother bishops in
the United States. To each of you and to all your local churches:
"Grace, mercy, and peace from God the Father and Christ Jesus
our Lord" (1 Tm 1:2).

Fourth Address of His Holiness
Pope John Paul II
to the Bishops of the United States
during Their *Ad Limina* Visits

June 10, 1988

Dear Brothers in our Lord Jesus Christ,

1. I extend a warm and fraternal greeting to all of you, pastors of the local churches in the provinces of Baltimore, Washington, Atlanta, and Miami.

It is a pleasure to note the presence of Archbishop Hickey in anticipation of the consistory in which he will be created a cardinal. In Archbishop Borders, I greet the first See of Baltimore as it prepares to celebrate next year its bicentennial, with profound significance for the whole Church in the United States. With particular fraternal affection, I send greetings to Archbishop Marino of Atlanta, the first black Archbishop in the United States, who will be arriving soon to receive the pallium. With gratitude, I reciprocate the cordial welcome given me by Archbishop McCarthy on my arrival in Miami. And to all of you, dear brothers in the episcopate, I express my esteem and solidarity in Christ Jesus.

I recently spoke to the bishops of Region V about the call to conversion, and on this occasion, I would like to speak to you about the call to prayer.

We have all meditated on the words of Jesus: "Pray constantly for the strength . . . to stand secure before the Son of Man" (Lk 21:36). And today, we accept once again the call to prayer as it comes to each of us and to the whole Church from Christ himself. The call to prayer places all the Church's activity in perspective. In 1976, in addressing the Call to Action meeting in Detroit, Paul VI stated that "in the tradition of the Church any call to action is first of all a call of prayer." These words are indeed more relevant today that ever before. They are a challenge to the Church in the United States and throughout the world.

2. The universal Church of Christ, and therefore each particular church, exists in order to pray. In prayer, the human person expresses

his or her nature; the community expresses its vocation; the Church reaches out to God. In prayer, the Church attains fellowship with the Father and with his Son, Jesus Christ (cf. 1 Jn 1:3). In prayer, the Church expresses her Trinitarian life because she directs herself to the Father, undergoes the action of the Holy Spirit, and lives fully her relationship with Christ. Indeed, she experiences herself as the Body of Christ, as the mystical Christ.

The Church meets Christ in prayer at the core of her being. It is in this way that she finds the complete relevance of his teaching and takes on his mentality. By fostering an interpersonal relationship with Christ, the Church actuates to the full the personal dignity of her members. In prayer, the Church concentrates on Christ; she possesses him, savors his friendship, and is, therefore, in a position to communicate him. Without prayer, all this would be lacking and she would have nothing to offer to the world. But by exercising faith, hope, and charity in prayer, her power to communicate Christ is reinforced.

3. Prayer is the goal of all catechesis in the Church because it is a means of union with God. Through prayer, the Church expresses the supremacy of God and fulfills the first and greatest commandment of love.

Everything human is profoundly affected by prayer. Human work is revolutionized by prayer, uplifted to its highest level. Prayer is the source of the full humanization of work. In prayer, the value of work is understood, for we grasp the fact that we are truly collaborators of God in the transformation and elevation of the world. Prayer is the consecration of this collaboration. At the same time, it is the means through which we face the problems of life and in which all pastoral endeavors are conceived and nurtured.

The call to prayer must precede the call to action, but the call to action must truly accompany the call to prayer. The Church finds in prayer the root of all her social action—the power to motivate it and the power to sustain it. In prayer, we discover the needs of our brothers and sisters and make them our own because, in prayer, we discover that their needs are the needs of Christ. All social consciousness is nurtured and evaluated in prayer. In the words of Jesus, justice and mercy are among "the weightier matters of the law" (Mt 23:23). The Church's struggle for justice and her pursuit of mercy will succeed only if the Holy Spirit gives her the gift of perseverance in attaining them. This gift must be sought in prayer.

4. In prayer, we come to understand the Beatitudes and the reasons why we must live them. Only through prayer can we begin

to see all the aspirations of humanity from the perspective of Christ. Without the intuitions of prayer, we would never grasp all the dimensions of human development and the urgency for the Christian community to commit itself to this work.

Prayer calls us to examine our consciences on all the issues that affect humanity. It calls us to ponder our personal and collective responsibility before the judgment of God and in the light of human solidarity. Hence, prayer is able to transform the world. Everything is new with prayer, both for individuals and communities. New goals and new ideas emerge. Christian dignity and action are reaffirmed. The commitments of our baptism, confirmation, and holy orders take on new urgency. The horizons of conjugal love and of the mission of the family are vastly extended in prayer.

Christian sensitivity depends on prayer. Prayer is an essential condition—even if not the only one—for a correct reading of the "signs of the times." Without prayer, deception is inevitable in a matter of such importance.

5. Decisions require prayer; decisions of magnitude require sustained prayer. Jesus himself gives us the example. Before calling his disciples and selecting the Twelve, Jesus passed the night on the mountain, in communion with his Father (cf. Lk 6:12). For Jesus, prayer to his Father meant not only light and strength. It also meant confidence, trust, and joy. His human nature exulted in the joy that came to him in prayer. The measure of the Church's joy in any age is in proportion to her prayer.

The gauge of her strength and the condition for her confidence are fidelity to prayer. The mysteries of Christ are disclosed to those who approach him in prayer. The full application of the Second Vatican Council will forever be conditioned by perseverance in prayer. The great strides made by the laity of the Church in realizing how much they belong to the Church—how much they are the Church—can only be explained in the last analysis by grace and its acceptance in prayer.

6. In the life of the Church today, we frequently perceive that the gift of prayer is linked to the word of God. A renewal in discovering the sacred Scriptures has brought forth the fruits of prayer. God's word, embraced and meditated on, has the power to bring human hearts into ever greater communion with the most Holy Trinity. Over and over again this has taken place in the Church in our day. The benefits received through prayer linked to the word of God call forth in all of us a further response of prayer—the prayer of praise and thanksgiving.

The word of God generates prayer in the whole community. At the same time, it is in prayer that the word of God is understood, applied, and lived. For all of us who are ministers of the Gospel, with the pastoral responsibility of announcing the message in season and out of season and of scrutinizing the reality of daily life in the light of God's holy word, prayer is the context in which we prepare the proclamation of faith. All evangelization is prepared in prayer; in prayer it is first applied to ourselves; in prayer it is then offered to the world.

7. Each local church is true to itself to the extent that it is a praying community with all the consequent dynamism that prayer stirs up within it. The universal Church is never more herself than when she faithfully reflects the image of the praying Christ: the Son who in prayer directs his whole being to his Father and consecrates himself for the sake of his brethren "that they may be consecrated in truth" (Jn 17:19).

For this reason, dear brothers in the episcopate, I wish to encourage you in all your efforts to teach people to pray. It is part of the apostolic Church to transmit the teaching of Jesus to each generation, to offer faithfully to each local church the response of Jesus to the request: "Teach us to pray" (Lk 11:1). I assure you of my solidarity and of the solidarity of the whole Church in your efforts to preach the importance of daily prayer and to give the example of prayer. From the words of Jesus, we know that where two or three are gathered in his name, there he is in their midst (cf. Mt 18:20). And we know that in every local church gathered in prayer around a bishop there dwells the incomparable beauty of the whole Catholic Church as the faithful image of the praying Christ.

8. In his role as pastor of the universal Church, the successor of Peter is called to live a communion of prayer with his brother bishops and their dioceses. Hence, all your pastoral initiatives to promote prayer have my full support. In fraternal and pastoral charity, I am close to you as you call your people to daily prayer, as you invite them to discover in prayer their dignity as Christians. Every diocesan and parish initiative aimed at furthering individual and family prayer is a blessing for the universal Church. Every group that gathers together to pray the rosary is a gift to the cause of God's kingdom. Yes, wherever two or three are gathered in Christ's name, there he is. Contemplative communities are a special gift of Christ's love to his people. They need and deserve the full measure of our pastoral love and support. Their particular role in the world is to bear witness to the supremacy of God and the

primacy of Christ's love "which surpasses all knowledge" (Eph 3:19).

When, as bishops, we exercise our apostolic responsibility to call our people to prayer, we also deeply fulfill our own pastoral ministry. Not everyone is waiting to be called to prayer; not everyone is willing to respond, but millions of people are. And the Holy Spirit is willing to use the bishops of the Church as instruments in a work that by reason of its supreme delicateness belongs to him alone as the *dextrae dei digitus*. The outpouring of the Holy Spirit can totally renew the Church today through the gift of prayer. We must aspire to possess this gift—so much linked to God's love; we must invoke it for the Church here and now and see it also as the hallmark of the Church of the millennium. This is the vital context in which, as pastors, we must call the Church to prayer. Here, too, we touch upon the identity of the bishop as a sign of Christ, "a sign of the praying Christ, a sign of the Christ who speaks to his Father, saying: 'I offer you praise, O Father, Lord of Heaven and Earth' (Lk 10:21)" (*Ad Limina* Address of December 3, 1983).

9. Prayer reaches a level of special dignity and efficacy for the community in the sacred liturgy of the Church and particularly in eucharistic worship, which is the source and summit of Christian living. In this regard, the eucharistic celebration of the Sunday is of immense importance for your local churches and for their vitality.

Five years ago, in speaking at some length about this matter, I mentioned that "throughout the United States there has been a superb history of eucharistic participation by the people, and for this we must all thank God" (*Ad Limina* Address of July 9, 1983). The time is ripe to renew gratitude to God for this great gift and to reinforce this splended tradition of American Catholics. On that occasion, I also mentioned: "All the striving of the laity to consecrate the secular field of activity to God finds inspiration and magnificent confirmation in the eucharistic sacrifice. Participating in the eucharist is only a small portion of the laity's week, but the total effectiveness of their lives and all Christian renewal depends on it: the primacy and indispensable source of the true Christian spirit!" (ibid.).

In their Sunday eucharistic assembly, the Father repeatedly glorifies the resurrection of his son Jesus Christ by accepting his sacrifice offered for the whole Church. He confirms the paschal character of the Church. The hour of Sunday eucharistic worship is a powerful expression of the Christocentric nature of the community, which Christ offers to his Father as a gift. And as he offers his

Church to his Father, Christ himself convokes his Church for her mission: her mission, above all of love and praise, to be able to say, "By your gift I will utter praise in the vast assembly" (Ps 22:26).

At the same time that the Church is summoned to praise, she is summoned to service in fraternal charity and in justice, mercy, and peace. In the very act of convoking his Church to service, Christ consecrates this service, renders it fruitful and offers it in the spirit to his Father. This service to which the Church is called is the service of evangelization and human advancement in all their vital aspects. It is service in the name of Christ and of his mercy, in the name of him who said, "My heart is moved with pity for the crowd" (Mt 15:32).

10. There are many other aspects of prayer, both private and liturgical, that deserve reflection. There are many other dimensions of the call to prayer that the Church would like to emphasize. I wish at this time, however, to allude only to two realities which the Church must constantly face and which she can face adequately only in prayer. They are suffering and sin.

It is in her prayer that the Church understands and copes with suffering; she reacts to it as Jesus did in the garden: "In his anguish he prayed with all the greater intensity" (Lk 22:44). Before the mystery of suffering, the Church is still unable to modify the advice of St. James or to improve on it: "Is anyone among you suffering? He should pray" (Jas 15:13). Combined with all her efforts to alleviate human suffering—which she must multiply until the end of time—the Church's definitive response to suffering is found only in prayer.

The other reality to which the Church responds in prayer is sin. In prayer, the Church braces herself to engage in paschal conflict with sin and with the devil. In prayer, she asks pardon for sin; in prayer, she implores mercy for sinners; and in prayer, she extols the power of the Lamb of God, who takes away the sins of the world. The Church's response to sin is to praise salvation and the superabundance of the grace of Jesus Christ, the savior of the world. "To him who loves us and freed us from our sins by his own blood . . . be glory and power forever and ever" (Rv 1:5-6).

Profoundly convinced of the power of prayer and humbly committed to it in our lives, let us, dear brothers, confidently proclaim throughout the Church the call to prayer. At stake is the Church's need to be herself, the Church of prayer, for the glory of the Father. The Holy Spirit will assist us, and the merits of Christ's paschal mystery will supply for our human weaknesses.

The example of Mary, the Mother of Jesus, as a model of prayer, is a source of confidence and trust for all of us. As we ourselves look to her, we know that her example sustains our clergy, religious, and laity. We know that her generosity is a legacy for the whole Church to proclaim and imitate.

Finally, in the words of Paul, I ask you all: "Pray for me that God may put his word on my lips, that I may courageously make known the mystery of the Gospel. . . . Pray that I may have courage to proclaim it as I ought. . . . Grace be with all who love our Lord Jesus Christ with unfailing love" (Eph 6:19-20, 24).

Fifth Address of His Holiness
Pope John Paul II
to the Bishops of the United States
during Their *Ad Limina* Visits

July 8, 1988

Dear Brothers in our Lord Jesus Christ,

1. Your welcome presence here today evokes the remembrance of all those events that we celebrated together in the provinces of Los Angeles and San Francisco during my pastoral visit last September.

Each event not only concerned the local church but involved the participation of many other people. Besides, there was the extensive spiritual presence of millions of the faithful. In this way, for example, I could address from San Francisco the whole Catholic laity and all the religious of the United States. The previous events in Los Angeles and Monterey likewise had a great significance for the direction that the Catholic Church must take in her own life and in her service to humanity, as she moves, under the action of the Holy Spirit, toward the purification so necessary for a proper celebration of the millennium. It would take a great deal of time to recall in detail all the events that we lived together in California. Although it is not possible to do so at this moment, I would request the Church in the United States to relive the commitment of those days and also renew her openness to the word of God as proclaimed by the successor of Peter in those situations. This attitude is necessary to ensure the success of an overall pastoral plan that must wisely guide the Church in your country in the years ahead.

2. One event of those days has a very special relevance now. It is the visit that I made to the Basilica of Carmel and to the tomb of Fray Junipero Serra. In less than three months from now, some of us will gather again here as the Church beatifies him, officially proclaiming him worthy of honor and imitation by all. In venerating "the Apostle of California" at his tomb, I spoke of his contribution, which was "to proclaim the Gospel of Jesus Christ at the dawn of

31

a new age" (September 17, 1987). I also endeavored to present his essential message, which is the constant need to evangelize. In that context I stated, "Like Father Serra and his Franciscan brethren, we, too, are called to be evangelizers, to share actively in the Church's mission of making disciples of all people."

Initial evangelization and continuing evangelization are pressing needs in the world today. As the Church pursues this task of hers—striving to relate the mystery of man to the mystery of God—she needs to have very clear ideas of her goal and the means by which she proposes to attain it. Of great help in all of this are the guiding principles and succinctly formulated intuitions of the Second Vatican Council. One of these truths so forcefully expressed by the council is "that only in the mystery of the Incarnate Word does the mystery of man take on light (*Gaudium et Spes*, 22). To understand humanity fully, including its dignity and its destiny, the world must understand Christ. Christ not only reveals God to man, but he also reveals man to himself. The mystery of humanity becomes comprehensible in the Incarnate Word. This principle becomes a guiding force for the Church in all her activities, which are directed to clarifying the mystery of humanity in the mystery of Christ.

3. Above all, this is true in catechesis, where the Church endeavors to lead the individual to a greater self-understanding through, in, and with Christ. To reach God, man must understand himself, and to do this he must look to Christ. The human being is created in the image and likeness of God. The full image of God is eternally found in Christ, whom St. Paul calls the "image of the invisible God" (Col 1:15).

As a creature, man is also a social being called to live in community with others. The highest form of community and interpersonal relation is that lived by Christ in the communion of the most Holy Trinity.

The human being further understands himself as made up of body and soul intimately united in one person. In Christ, there are hypostatically united in the one divine person both the human and the divine natures. Man's wonderful destiny is to share, through Christ's humanity, in his divine nature (cf. 2 Pt 1:4). Man is called to glorify God in his body and treat his body in a way worthy of its dignity. In Jesus himself there dwells, bodily, the fullness of divinity (cf. Col 2:9). Through his intellect, man surpasses the whole of the material universe and comes into contact with the divine truth. Jesus as the Incarnate Word claimed in all exactness to be identified with that truth, when he said: "I am the way, and the truth and the life" (Jn 14:6).

By the action of the Holy Spirit, man is in a position to know the plan of God, as regards both creation and redemption. Jesus himself is that plan of God: "Through him all things come into being, and apart from him nothing came to be" (Jn 1:3). Moreover, we know that God has made him "our wisdom and also our justice, our sanctification and our redemption" (1 Cor 1:30).

In coming to know himself, man detects in the depth of his conscience a law which he does not impose upon himself, but which holds him in obedience (cf. *Gaudium et Spes,* 16). Jesus himself reveals the fullness and essence of all law, which is summarized in the love of God and the love of neighbor (cf. Mt 22:37-40). To love in the way that Jesus commands is the only way to satisfy fully the human heart.

Authentic freedom is a special sign of God's image in man. Jesus the man embodies the highest form of human freedom, by which he consecrates his life and his death to his Father and lives totally according to his will. He declares that his freedom is for his Father when he says, "I always do what pleases him" (Jn 8:29). At the same time, Jesus destroys what is opposed to freedom in the human person. His mission is to cast out the one who holds man's conscience in bondage.

The final riddle for human beings is death. In looking to Christ, man learns that he himself is destined to live. Christ's eucharist is the pledge of life. The one who eats Christ's flesh and drinks his blood already has eternal life (cf. Jn 6:54). Finally, in conquering death by his resurrection, Christ reveals the resurrection of all; he proclaims life and reveals man to himself in his final destiny, which is life.

Of supreme relevance for the Church today is the presentation of the person of the Incarnate Word as the center of all catechesis. Some years ago, in 1971, in accord with the council's decree *Christus Dominus,* the Congregation for the Clergy issued the *General Catechetical Directory* for the Church. Its aim was to promote a Christocentric catechesis for all the people of God. In doing this it stated, "Catechesis must proclaim Jesus in his concrete existence and in his message, that is, it must open the way for man to the wonderful perfection of his humanity" (53).

Eight years later, I endeavored to give impetus to this Christocentric approach to catechesis by the publication of *Catechesi Tradendae.* In this document I said: "At the heart of catechesis we find, in essence, a person, the person of Jesus of Nazareth. . . . The primary and essential object of catechesis is . . . 'the mystery of Christ.' Catechizing is a way to lead a person to study this mystery in all its dimensions. . . . It is therefore to reveal in the person of Christ the whole of God's eternal design, reaching fulfillment in that person. . . . Accordingly, the definitive aim of catechesis is to put people not only in touch but in communion, in intimacy, with Jesus Christ" (5).

This important effort toward Christocentric catechesis, so fully dealt with in the synod of 1977 and in the apostolic exhortation to which I have alluded, has also become the guiding principle in the preparation of a universal catechism for serving the common needs of the Church. This document is meant to be a point of reference for all the catechetical efforts at the national and diocesan levels, and also for catechisms of a general and special nature which the bishops may subsequently draft with the purpose of imparting proper knowledge of the content of the Catholic faith. At the center of this effort is the profound conviction that the mystery of the Incarnate Word sheds light on all life and human experience and that he himself is in a position personally to communicate the truth that he is. Once again, in the words of *Catechesi Tradendae*: "We must therefore say that in catechesis it is Christ the Incarnate Word and Son of God who is taught—everything else is taught with reference to him—and it is Christ alone who teaches—anyone else teaches to the extent that he is Christ's spokesman, enabling Christ to speak with his lips" (6).

What Christ teaches is the truth that he is, in himself and for us. He reminds us, "My teaching is not mine, but his who sent me" (Jn 7:16). He speaks as the revelation of the Father, the blueprint of all creation, the creating word of God. In revealing the Father to humanity, Jesus reveals in himself how the Father looks upon humanity. He reveals God's plan for human nature in all its expressions and applications. Human love and human work participates in the divine model of uncreated and creating love. Procreation is a special participation in that divine prerogative. The authenticity and finality of human sexuality, justice, and freedom are found in the eternal plan of God expressed in Christ.

5. As pastors of the Church, you are daily experiencing, especially in the case of migrants and immigrants, the tragic and pressing problems of poverty. You have repeatedly called your people to a sense of solidarity with those in need. You have stood by all those who are struggling to live in a way consonant with their human

dignity. You are able to affirm from personal knowledge that "the powerful and almost irresistible aspiration that people have for liberation constitutes one of the principle signs of the times which the Church has to examine and interpret in the light of the Gospel" (*Instruction on Certain Aspects of the Theology of Liberation*, August 6, 1984, 1:1). At the same time, you have experienced how the quest for freedom and the aspiration to liberation, which are universal and yet differ in form and degree among peoples, have their source and impetus in the Christian heritage. In 1979, in the context of Puebla, I proposed three basic truths to orient all the efforts of the Church aimed at liberating and uplifting those in need. These are the truths about Jesus Christ, the truth about the Church, the truth about humanity. In effect, however, the truth about the Church and humanity is to be pondered in the light of the mystery of Jesus Christ, the Incarnate Word.

The same can be said of all dimensions of the human and Christian life. God's providence is understood only in conjunction with the eternal destiny of the human person as revealed by the Incarnate Word. The full meaning of human progress or development must take into account Christ's teaching: "Not on bread alone is man to live but on every utterance that comes from the mouth of God" (Mt 4:4; cf. Dt 8:3). The imperfections of human justice and the inadequacy of all earthly fulfillment are ultimately linked to God's design revealed in Christ that "here we have no lasting city, but seek one that is to come" (Heb 13:14). The question of physical and spiritual suffering on the part of the innocent requires an explanation that only the Incarnate Word could give. And in order to give it as effectively as possible, he gave it from the cross.

6. In your ministry as bishops, you constantly come across the complicated phenomena of *agnosticism* and *atheism*. You are rightly convinced of the need for sustained dialogue and fraternal collaboration in projects of service to humanity. You and your local churches are committed to giving an explanation for the hope that is in Christianity every time you are asked. You rightly count on the power of example and prayer; you know the need for patience and persevering trust. The great illuminating force, however, for all doubting and denying consciences, is only the light of the Incarnate Word which is for them, too, like "a lamp shining in a dark place until the first streaks of dawn appear and the morning star rises" (2 Pt 1:19).

In facing atheism, which the council says is "among the most serious problems of this age" (*Gaudium et Spes*, 19), and which is manifested in phenomena that are quite distinct from one another, the Church must also accept the judgment of the council that "believers can have more than a little to do with the birth of atheism" (ibid.). This is so to the extent that they fail to reveal the authentic face of God and religion—which is found in the Incarnate Word.

7. In directing the minds and the hearts of the faithful to the mystery of the Incarnate Word, the Church ardently desires to bring this mystery to bear on all human activity, all human culture. The Church, in effect, desires the birth of new humanism, profoundly Christian in its inspiration, in which earthly reality in its totality will be elevated by the revelation of Christ. One of the first characteristics of this new humanism is that it marks the community by a sense of interdependance expressed in solidarity. This is in accordance with Christ's intention to save humanity not merely as individuals, without mutual bonds, but to gather them into a single people (cf. *Lumen Gentium*, 9; *Gaudium et Spes*, 32). The Second Vatican Council already perceived the existence of this reality when it stated, "Thus we are witnesses of the birth of a new humanism, one in which man is defined first of all by his responsibility toward his brothers and sisters and toward history" (*Gaudium et Spes*, 55). Only with a consciousness of interdependence—pushed into a worldwide dimension—will communities unite to cultivate those natural goods and values that foster the well-being of humanity and constitute its basic culture.

The response of every community, including those in the Church, to a consciousness of interdependence is the excercise of solidarity, which is "a firm and persevering determination to commit oneself to the common good" (*Sollicitudo Rei Socialis*, 38). In turn, this solidarity or determination is expressed in a new moral concern for all the problems faced by humanity. Two extremely relevant problems faced by millions of our brothers and sisters throughout the world are development and peace (cf. ibid., 26). The outcome of these issues is profoundly affected by the way these realities are conceived in the context of a true Christian humanism.

The specific contribution of the Church—of her members and of her individual communities—to the cause of a new humanism, of true human culture, is the full truth of Christ about humanity: the meaning of humanity, its origin, its destiny, and, therefore, its incomparable dignity.

8. Dear Brother Bishops: Yours is a great task to guide, in union with the universal Church, your local churchs in the way of salva-

tion and with fraternal and paternal love to help the different categories of the faithful to fulfill their duty and privilege of bearing witness to Christ in the world. But you must also remember—and this will bring you great joy—that you are the principal communicators of Christ, the principal catechists of your people, the principal heralds of the mystery of the Incarnate Word. To you and to all your brothers in the college of bishops, united with the successor of Peter, there has been entrusted, in a unique way, for faithful custody and effective transmission, the truth of the Gospel. This truth we proclaim not only as salvation and deliverance from evil, but also as the basis of that new humanism which will speak to the whole world about universal solidarity and loving concern for all human beings.

All of this stems, dear brothers, from that profound conviction and principle enunciated by the Second Vatican Council: "The truth is that only in the light of the Incarnate Word does the mystery of man take on light." In the footsteps of your own "Apostle of California," and in solidarity with all your evangelizing predecessors, may you continue to proclaim confidently up and down El Camino Real, and beyond, the mystery of the Incarnate Word. In his love, I send my blessing to all the priests, deacons, religious, seminarians, and laity of California, Hawaii, and Nevada. "Peace to all of you who are in Christ (1 Pt 5:14)."

Sixth Address of His Holiness
Pope John Paul II
to the Bishops of the United States
during Their *Ad Limina* Visits

September 2, 1988

Dear Brothers in our Lord Jesus Christ,

1. With deep fraternal affection, I welcome all of you, the bishops of Regions XII and XIII. Our meeting today is meant to be not only an experience in ecclesial communion for us as pastors of God's people, but also a renewed commitment on the part of all the dioceses in the provinces of Anchorage, Portland, Seattle, Denver, and Santa Fe to that unity which Christ wills between the particular churches and the universal Church.

At this moment, our program calls us to reflect together on our ministry and on the profound pastoral solicitude that we as bishops must have for humanity and for every human being. To be authentic, our episcopal ministry must truly be centered on man. At the same time, it must be centered on God, whose absolute primacy and supremacy we must constantly proclaim and urge our people to recognize in their lives.

The Second Vatican Council has invited us to adopt both of these approaches—*anthropocentrism* and *theocentrism*—and to emphasize them together, linking them in the only satisfactory way possible, that is, in the divine person of Christ, true God and true man. This task for us is both formidable and exhilarating. The effect it can have on the local churches is profound. In my encyclical on God's mercy I stated that the deep and organic linking of anthropocentrism and theocentrism in Jesus Christ is perhaps the most important principle of the Second Vatican Council (*Dives in Misericordia*, 1). The basic reason for this is the pastoral effectiveness of this principle.

2. In concentrating on Christ, the Church is able to exalt human nature and human dignity, for Jesus Christ is the ultimate confirmation of all human dignity. The Church is also able to concentrate

on humanity and on the well-being of each human being because of the fact that in the Incarnation, Jesus Christ united all humanity to himself. In Christ, God the Father has placed the blueprint of humanity. At the same time, in concentrating on Christ, the Church emphasizes the centrality of God in the world, for in Christ—through the hypostatic union—God has taken possession of man to the greatest possible degree.

To proclaim Christ to the full extent willed by the Second Vatican Council is to exalt man supremely and to exalt God supremely. To proclaim Christ fully is to proclaim him in the Father's plan of the Incarnation, which expresses man's greatest glory and God's greatest accomplishment in the world. Anthropocentrism and theocentrism truly linked in Christ open the way for the Church to a proper understanding of her pastoral service to humanity, for the glory of God.

3. As the lawgiver of the New Testament, Christ links in his own person the two commandments of love of God and love of neighbor. While maintaining for the Church the priority of love of God, St. Augustine clarifies its order of fulfillment: "Loving God comes first as a commandment, but loving one's neighbor comes first as a deed" (*"Dei dilectio prior est ordine praecipiendi, proximi autem dilectio prior est ordine faciendi"*) (tract. *In Ioannem*, 17). In this sense, St. John's words remain a lasting challenge to the Church: "One who has no love for the brother he has seen cannot love the God he has not seen" (Jn 4:20).

In Christ—in his person and in his word—the Church discovers the principle of her solicitude for humanity (cf. *Redemptor Hominis*, 15). Her inspiration and her strength in all dimensions of her pastoral service are found in Christ. With a view to serving man, the Church will always reflect on him in relationship to Christ, and she will endeavor to approach God only through Christ. From this viewpoint, it is possible to hold that "man is the primary route that the Church must travel in fulfilling her mission; he is the primary and fundamental way for the Church" (ibid., 14). At the same time, without contradiction we proclaim that "Jesus Christ is the chief way for the Church" (ibid., 10). This is so because Christ is the fullness of humanity. Christ is God's expression of what humanity is meant to be, how humanity is meant to be transformed, how humanity is meant to be introduced into the communion of the Blessed Trinity, namely: "through him, and with him, and in him."

4. In speaking here of anthropocentrism, that is, in emphasizing the dignity of humanity in relation to Christ and to the Church's

mission, it is necessary to make reference to the immutable basis of all Christian anthropology, which is creation in the image and likeness of God (cf. Gn 1:26-27). This God is the God who reveals himself as a communion of persons, a saving God, a God of love and mercy.

In the Church's solicitude for man and for human dignity, which finds expression in every social program initiated by her, the Church must proclaim the reality of creation as it is renewed by the redemption and by the uplifting—effected in baptism—of each individual person. In her inner being, the Church feels impelled to proclaim human dignity: the dignity of man raised to the level of Christ, to the level of divine adoption. Hence, with the proclamation of natural human dignity, the Church also proclaims full Christian dignity: the dignity of the children of God called to a supernatural dignity, called to worship the Father with Christ.

In speaking to the American bishops five years ago, I made reference to "the pastoral service of making God's people ever more conscious of their dignity as a people of worship" (Address of July 9, 1983, no. 8). In particular, I noted "that we can render a great pastoral service to the people by emphasizing their liturgical dignity and by directing their thoughts to the purposes of worship. When our people . . . realize that they are called . . . to adore and thank the Father in union with Jesus Christ, an immense power is unleashed in their Christian lives" (ibid., no. 3).

With regard to rights within the Church, Pope John Paul I, ten years ago, on the occasion of one of the two *ad limina* visits of his short pontificate—on the very day he died—spoke in these terms: "Among the rights of the faithful, one of the greatest is the right to receive God's word in all its entirety and purity, with all its exigencies and power" (September 28, 1978). Under every aspect, the Church is irrevocably committed to the vigorous defense of all human and Christian rights, both in themselves and especially when these rights are threatened. With the realization that she lives in anticipation of the fullness of the kingdom of God, she must pursue constantly the work of the Messiah, of whom the psalmist says: "He shall have pity on the lowly and the poor; the lives of the poor he shall save. From fraud and violence he shall redeem them" (Ps 72:13-14). The Church must then always be at home among the poor, vigilant in the defense of all their rights.

5. In giving us the basis for the defense of human rights, Christ proclaims a whole structure of human relationships. He teaches us that to save our life we must lose it (cf. Lk 17:33). Indeed, the human

being cannot fully find himself without first making a sincere gift of self (cf. *Gaudium et Spes*, 24). This is so because to be a person in the image and likeness of God is to exist in relation to another and to others.

What Christ and his Church advocate is not the mere external defense of human rights, nor the mere defense of human rights by the organisms and structures at the disposal of the community—however providential and useful these may be—but the total commitment of giving on the part of each individual in the community so that the rights of all may be ensured through the great structure of proper human and Christian relationships in which the charity of Christ reigns supreme and in which justice is "corrected" by love (cf. *Dives in Misericordia*, 14). This structure of personal relationships—the only one conducive to the full defense of human and Christian rights—must view the human being as created in the image and likeness of God as God exists: a communion of persons.

6. A phenomenon that militates against this whole structure of personal relationships and, therefore, against human rights, a phenomenon that I have brought to the attention of the whole Church is "the decline of many fundamental values, values that constitute an unquestionable good not only for Christian morality but simply for human morality, for moral culture: these values include respect for human life from the moment of conception, respect for marriage in its indissoluble unity, and respect for the stability of the family. . . . Hand in hand with this go the crisis of truth in human relationships, lack of responsibility for what one says, the purely utilitarian relationship between individual and individual, the loss of a sense of the authentic common good and the ease with which this good is alienated" (ibid., 12). Each one of these areas would merit to be developed at length. In the past, I have spoken to you in some detail on some of these topics. I am profoundly grateful to you for your persevering efforts in so many pastoral challenges, one of the greatest being the defense and support of human life.

7. A major area of human rights in need of constant defense is that concerned with the family and its members, both parents and children. The *Charter of the Rights of the Family*, presented five years ago by the Holy See, has spelled out these rights and deserves renewed attention at this time. One of the fundamental principles enunciated in this document is "the original, primary and inalienable right" of parents to educate their children (art. 5) according to their moral and religious convictions and to supervise closely and to control their sex education. The Church must continue to present

human sexuality as linked to God's plan of creation and constantly proclaim the finality and dignity of sex.

Ways by which the human family is greatly wounded include the unsolved problems of immensely lucrative drug trafficking and pornography. Both of these plague society, debase human life and human love, and violate human rights.

8. In dealing with the specific rights of women as women, it is necessary to return again and again to the immutable basis of Christian anthropology as it is foreshadowed in the scriptural account of the creation of man—as male and female—in the image and likeness of God. Both man and woman are created in the image of the personhood of God, with inalienable personal dignity, and in complementarity—one with the other. Whatever violates the complementarity of women and men, whatever impedes the true communion of persons according to the complementarity of the sexes offends the dignity of both women and men.

Through the first draft of your proposed document on the concerns of women for the Church and society, I know that you are making real efforts to respond with sensitivity to these greatly varying concerns by presenting women as partners in the mystery of the redemption, as this mystery is lived out in our day. You are rightly striving to help eliminate discrimination based on sex. You are also rightly presenting Mary, the Mother of God, as a model of discipleship and a sign of hope to all and, at the same time, as a special symbol and model for women in their partnership with God in the ministry of the Church.

Throughout the whole Church, a great prayerful reflection still remains to be made on the teaching of the Church about women and about their dignity and vocation. I have already announced my own intention to publish a document on this subject, and this document will come out shortly. The Church is determined to place her full teaching, with all the power with which divine truth is invested, at the service of the cause of women in the modern world—to help clarify their correlative rights and duties, while defending their feminine dignity and vocation. The importance of true Christian feminism is so great that every effort must be made to present the principles on which this cause is based, and according to which it can be effectively defended and promoted for the good of all humanity. The seriousness of this commitment requires the collaboration not only of the entire college of bishops but also of the whole Church.

9. The status of all human dignity and all human rights is immeasurably enhanced by the supernatural condition and destiny of humanity, which are found only in relation to God, only in relation to Christ. Paul VI, in his powerful social encyclical, *Populorum Progressio (On the Development of Peoples)*, wanted to present these elements together. He wanted the Church to follow a course of social action that would be solidly secure. In other words, he wanted to link human rights and dignity—indeed, the whole of humanism—to God, in Christ. In a word, he wanted to insist that the Church can and must be both anthropocentric and theocentric at the same time, by being Christocentric, by concentrating on Christ, the Redeemer of man, the Redeemer of all humanity. This message of his is more important now than ever before for our people, namely, that "by union with Christ man attains to new fulfillment of himself, to a transcendent humanism that gives him his greatest possible perfection" (16). And again: "There is no true humanism but that which is open to the absolute and is conscious of a vocation which gives human life its true meaning" (ibid., 42). For all of us, this vocation is the Christian vocation—essentially linked to the Incarnation and to the cause of human dignity and human rights as they are incomparably spelled out by the Incarnate Word.

And when human justice is not only practiced but "corrected" by love, the cause of all humanity is immeasurably enriched. Through the charity of Christ, the Incarnate Word, the horizons of service—exercised in the name of the Gospel and of the mission of the Church—are vastly extended.

As pastors of God's people, dear brothers, we have known from experience how relevant all these principles are at every level of the Church, in every community of the faithful, no matter how small or how large. There is no other path to take than man and human dignity. There is no other direction in which to point him than to God. There is no other way to arrive than through Christ. In building up the kingdom of God, there is no other cause than the cause of humanity understood in the light of Christ, who says: "as often as you did it for one of my least brothers, you did it for me" (Mt 25:40).

With these reflections, dear brothers, I assure you of my prayers that all your local churches will ever increasingly find in Christ the everlasting link between the cause of humanity and the kingdom of God, and that in Christ, they will experience inspiration and strength for their lives. May God reward you for your own zeal and generosity and for all the pastoral love with which you serve his holy people. With my apostolic blessing.

Seventh Address of His Holiness
Pope John Paul II
to the Bishops of the United States
during Their *Ad Limina* Visits

September 9, 1988

Dear Brothers in Christ,

1. For the seventh time this year, I have the joy of welcoming to the See of Peter my brother bishops from the United States on their *ad limina* visit. In you, the bishops of Regions I and VIII, I greet all the beloved Catholic people who make up the Church in New England and in the states if Minnesota, North Dakota, and South Dakota. I realize that there are great differences between your regions and in the makeup of your local churches, but I know that you all experience common challenges in living the one, holy, catholic, and apostolic faith.

During the previous visits, I had the occasion to reflect with the bishops on the pastoral mission of the Church. All my discourses were aimed at helping them to lead their ecclesial communities to live the life of faith as fully as possible. In this way, I was able to treat a series of topics that are relevant for all the dioceses in America: the mystery of the Church as it exists in the United States—the wonderful reality of God's grace that I was able to witness personally and that must constantly be called to ever greater heights of holiness; the preparation required for the millennium, as a period of special renewal of the Church in her identity and mission; the call to penance and reconciliation; the call to prayer; reflection on Jesus Christ as the one who communicates the mystery of God and reveals man to himself; and, finally, the organic linking in Christ of all the anthropocentric and theocentric efforts of the Church, including her role of proclaiming human dignity and human rights. Today, dear brothers, I would like to add to this series by reflecting on the consciousness that the Church in the United States must have of her mission of solidarity with all humanity.

2. The Church, like the individual human beings who are her members, is strong in the act of giving (cf. *Gaudium et Spes*, 24).

Like the human person, the ecclesial community finds itself in reaching out and in sharing the gift of itself. Solidarity is the expression of the Church's life and of her dynamism in Christ. Such solidarity involves a practical awareness of the great network of interdependence that exists among God's people. It consists in a firm and persevering commitment to the good of all (cf. *Sollicitudo Rei Socialis*, 38).

As the Body of Christ, the Church discovers and puts into practice solidarity at the level of divine mystery, at every level of her catholicity, and at every level of human need. All the particular churches that make up the one Catholic Church are called to live the same universal solidarity with their sister churches, in an awareness of the one catholic communion that unites them in the mission of Christ. Each local church expresses this interdependence in faith and love and in whatever touches the lives of human beings. Each local church perceives its interdependence in the need to be open to others and learn from them, as well as by helping them to bear their burdens according to the expression of St. Paul: "Help carry one another's burdens; in that way you will fulfill the law of Christ" (Gal 6:2). Wherever, throughout the universal Church, the faithful experience need, there the response of solidarity is called for. For the Church, solidarity is the expression of the catholicity of her being as she reaches out to all her sons and daughters in need.

3. Precisely because she is the Church, she is called to embrace all humanity in need, to respond to the needs of all people. The Church clearly acknowledges and proclaims universal interdependence and the interrelation of human needs. In your pastoral letters on peace and on economic justice, you as a conference expressed these points well, when you said: "Since we profess to be members of a 'catholic' or universal Church, we all must raise our sights to a concern for the well-being of everyone in the world. . . . We commit ourselves to this global vision" (*Economic Justice for All*, 363). And again: "The interdependence of the world means a set of interrelated human questions. Important as keeping the peace in the nuclear age is, it does not solve or dissolve the other major problems of the day" (*The Challenge of Peace*, 259).

For the Church, solidarity is a moral and social attitude to be cultivated, a virtue to be practiced, a duty to be expressed in many forms of fraternal assistance and collaboration. As far as solidarity in social progress is concerned, the Church has seen the need in recent decades to emphasize the worldwide dimension. It is this worldwide dimension or universal character of the Church's social

46

teaching that characterized *Mater et Magistra, Gaudium et Spes,* and *Populorum Progressio,* and now it has been further explored in my own encyclical, *Sollicitudo Rei Socialis.* To cite Paul VI in this regard: "Today the principal fact that we must all recognize is that the social question has become worldwide" (*Populorum Progressio,* 3).

4. Solidarity is relevant in itself as a human and Christian virtue, but it is further relevant in its relationship to peace. It is indeed a factor of peace in the modern world, and when it includes solidarity in truth, freedom, justice, and love, it becomes the firm basis for a new world order. Solidarity is a factor of peace because it is crucial for development: "There can be no progress toward the complete development of man without the simultaneous development of all humanity in the spirit of solidarity" (ibid., 43).

It is important for the Church to realize that she exercises solidarity with the whole world as an expression of her own ecclesial life. Her social concern, like her evangelizing zeal, knows no barriers, precisely because she is the Church, "a kind of sacrament of intimate union with God, and of the unity of all mankind, that is, she is a sign and an instrument of such union and unity" (*Lumen Gentium,* 1).

At the same time, the Church willingly exercises solidarity with an ecumenical and interreligious dimension, which she considers extremely important. She lives to serve—like Christ—the cause of humanity: "The Son of Man has not come to be served but to serve—to give his life in ransom for many" (Mk 10:45). The Church also knows that she must imitate the sensitivity of Christ for humanity; she frequently recalls his words: "My heart is moved with pity for the crowd" (Mt 15:3).

5. With this sensitivity, the Church is called to understand and face a multiplicity of needs that differ among themselves, demonstrating her solidarity and offering her help according to her means and her specific nature. This great openness to others has been characteristic of the Church in the United States. It is a gift of God implanted in the hearts of your people; it must be nurtured, maintained, reflected upon, acted upon. During my first visit to the United States in 1979, I spoke to the bishops at Chicago in these terms: "An evident concern for others has been a real part of American Catholicism, and today I thank the American Catholics for their generosity. . . . For me this is an hour of solemn gratitude" (October 5, 1979, no. 1). I express these sentiments once more.

The solidarity about which we speak is that genuine solidarity that is expressed in a spirit of sharing, accompanied by real human feeling, and motivated by supernatural charity. It is a social concern that embraces all men, women, and children in the totality of their personhood, which comprises their human rights, their condition in this world, and their eternal destiny. We cannot prescind from any of these elements. It is a solidarity that accepts and emphasizes the equality of basic human dignity and translates itself into Christian prayer, according to the formula of Jesus: "Our Father . . . give us this day our daily bread."

All human needs enter into the Church's concern and call for involvement on the part of her members. As I have stated, collaboration is the act proper to solidarity (cf. *Sollicitudo Rei Socialis*, 39), and both solidarity and collaboration are means of defending human rights and serving the truth and freedom of humanity. How wonderful is the solidarity that has grown up in the United States today among so many men and women of good will who are pledged to the defense and service of human life! How effectively they contribute to that great American ideal of "liberty and justice for all!"

Solidarity is a response to Christ's challenge, and while it is carried out in the name of Christ and his Church, it is done without distinction of creed, sex, race, nationality, or political affiliation. The final aim can only be the human being in need.

6. Among the positive signs of a new moral concern in the world— a concern that is increasing among the Catholic people in the United States—are not only a renewed awareness of human dignity but also a conviction of the basic interdependence of all humanity, especially in facing poverty and underdevelopment. Consequently, there is a growing consciousness that peace is indivisible and that true development is either shared by all or it is not true development (cf. *Sollicitudo Rei Socialis*, 17). From this point of view, we see how important economic and commercial relations are among the countries and peoples of the world and how important it is that justice be observed in this sector.

As pastors of God's people, you have asked them to reflect on both the indivisibility of peace and on the consequences of economic interdependence. You have stated that "all of us must confront the reality of such economic bonding and its consequences and see it as a moment of grace . . . that can unite all of us in a common community of the human family" (*Economic Justice for All*, 363).

7. The twentieth anniversary of *Populorum Progressio* offered the whole Church the opportunity to reflect further on the meaning and content of true human development as it affects individuals and all people. This reflection will continue in the Church because

of the importance of this theme as it relates to her mission of service in the name of Christ. The integral, interior, and transcendent dimensions of human progress merit attention, as do the economic, social, and cultural indices of underdevelopment and poverty.

My latest encyclical attempted to place renewed emphasis on the transcendent reality of the human being and thus spell out again the meaning of authentic development in terms of the specific nature of man. Many conclusions supporting human dignity flow from these principles. Underdevelopment in all its forms is more easily identified and combated when the true nature of development is known. The distinction between *being* and *having* is still essential in understanding genuine progress. For this reason, Paul VI pointed out that the exclusive pursuit of possessions is a real obstacle to development and that "avarice is the most evident form of moral underdevelopment" (*Populorum Progressio,* 19). Considering how important human rights are to the human person, it is clear that they must be vigorously defended in every program of development. To this end, all the resources of human solidarity must be mobilized. It is evident that individual efforts are insufficient. Concentrated efforts must be made to identify true progress and to ensure its attainment by all through universal solidarity.

8. Areas of special social concern are poverty and underdevelopment. On the international level, the underdevelopment of peoples is accompanied and aggravated by the immense problem of their countries' debts. The individual issues of hunger, homelessness, unemployment, and underemployment are formidable and call for the creative collaboration of each ecclesial community.

One extraordinary example of the creative solidarity of American Catholics is Catholic Relief Services, founded by the American bishops in 1943 to help meet urgent needs in Europe and North Africa. Subsequently, and with equal creativity, the organization responded, on behalf of the Catholic Church in the United States, to other needs throughout the world, and it is still known today as "the official overseas aid and development agency of American Catholics." This organization, which has done so much in the past, and which is still so needed for real services in the world today, exists as a result of the application of the principles on which we have been reflecting.

In the case of Catholic Relief Services, the American bishops conceived and constituted a whole ecclesial program on the basis of the principles of interdependence, solidarity, and collaboration, to be carried out with keen human sensitivity and the full power of

Christian charity. The supreme motivation for solidarity—for the Church and all her institutions—will remain the love that God has in Christ for all humanity: "God so loved the world that he gave his only Son" (Jn 3:16).

9. Side by side with all her social concerns there is and always must be the response of the Church to the even higher needs of humanity. Her religious mission impels the Church, in season and out of season, to repeat with Jesus: "Not on bread alone is man to live but on every utterance that comes from the mouth of God" (Jn 4:4; cf. Dt 8:3). Like the Incarnate Word—and until he comes again in glory—the Church must continue to show her solidarity with all humanity, being conscious of the central fact of history that "the Word became flesh" (Jn 1:14).

Dear Brothers: In the love of Christ, I send my greetings and blessing to all your local churches as they find strength and practice solidarity in his name.

Eighth Address of His Holiness
Pope John Paul II
to the Bishops of the United States
during Their *Ad Limina* Visits

October 7, 1988

Dear Brothers in our Lord Jesus Christ,

1. In you, the bishops of Region III, I greet with deep pastoral love all the people of God in the states of New Jersey and Pennsylvania. During your *ad limina* visit, the bonds of hierarchical communion are being strengthened between the bishop of Rome and his brothers in the episcopate, together with their local churches. At the same time, the horizon of our pastoral service opens wide to view the Church as "a sign and instrument of intimate union with God and of the unity of the whole human race" (*Lumen Gentium*, 1).

In this context, we are called to renew our zeal for the unity of all Christians as well as our openness to those who profess other religions and, indeed, to all people of good will. This is the reflection that I would now like to make with you.

Our faith in the Church is inseparable from our profession that Jesus is "the Christ, the Son of the living God" (Mt 16:16). The mysterious communion between God and man in Christ is prolonged in the Church. The Church is the fruit of that hypostatic union which achieved its full redeeming efficacy in the paschal mystery. And the Church is the means that the Holy Spirit uses to incorporate all people into Christ by incorporating them into the Church. Indeed, the Church belongs to the work of redemption. In Christ, she is throughout all history the instrument of saving communion which is open to all humanity.

There is a close relationship between the temporal and visible ecclesial communion and the eternal and invisible communion of the most Holy Trinity. They are not parallel realities. As the Second Vatican Council says, citing St. Cyprian, the Church is "made one with the unity of the Father and the Son and the Holy Spirit" (ibid.,

4). The communion of the Blessed Trinity is the source from which is derived the communion with God. With deep faith, the Second Vatican Council teaches that "this pilgrim Church is necessary for salvation" (ibid., 14).

2. A great love of God's plan of salvation in Christ and the conviction of the necessity of the Church are at the root of that zealous sense of mission which should animate all Catholics. Opposed to this zeal is the relativism which would deny the unique value of Christ's Gospel and his Church. To offer Christ and his message to the world will always be a challenge to Christian fidelity and pastoral wisdom.

If we are convinced—and we are—that Christ is the fullness of truth; if we profess—and we do—that the Church has been instituted by Christ for the salvation of all, then to be consistent we will want to engage constantly in the dialogue of salvation, so that as many as possible may find joy in the good news of God's merciful love revealed in his Son, Jesus Christ.

Since it is charity that spurs us on in our task, we will carry out this mission with prayer, good example, and sacrifice—with a charity that expresses itself in genuine respect for the beliefs of others. Zeal for the Gospel of Christ, which should characterize all of the faithful, leads us to understand, to forgive, and to respect the action of God's grace which works through human freedom. We do not subject people to pressure or offend anyone when we follow in Christ's footsteps and travel the path of self-denial and service that began in Bethlehem, was consummated on the cross, and reaches us in the eucharist.

3. It is also necessary to increase unity and fraternal love among Catholics. This is essential if our ecumenical zeal is to be credible: "This is how all will know that you are my disciples, if you have love for one another" (Jn 13:35). As my predecessor, Paul VI, so clearly said at the time of the council: "The unity of the Church must be received and recognized by each and every member of the Church, and it must be promoted, loved and defended by each and every member of the Church. It is not enough to call oneself a Catholic. We must be truly united." And he continued: "Today people speak a great deal about reestablishing unity with our separated brethren, and this is good. This is a very worthwhile endeavor, and we all ought to cooperate in it with humility, tenacity and confidence. But we must not forget our duty to work even more for the Church's internal unity, which is so necessary for her spiritual and apostolic vitality" (General Audience, March 31, 1965).

On the occasion of our meeting today, dear brothers, when there is manifest a *communio* which is both affective and effective, I cannot but repeat what the council said about our role in this regard: "The Roman pontiff, as the successor of Peter, is the perpetual and visible principle and foundation of unity of both the bishops and of the faithful. The individual bishops, however, are the visible principle and foundation of unity in their particular churches" (*Lumen Gentium*, 23). May all of us work together to foster the inner unity of the Church, which is the will of Christ and which also guarantees the effectiveness of our ecumenical efforts.

4. Within the Catholic Church herself, we have to live the well-known maxim: *"In necessariis unitas, in dubiis libertas, in omnibus caritas"* ("In necessary things, unity; in doubtful things, freedom; in all things, charity"). In this way, we can properly combine unity with diversity and ensure the necessary climate of freedom within the ecclesial community. This principle sustains the common patrimony of faith and moral teaching while leaving options in theological studies, spirituality, means of evangelization, and ways of infusing the Christian spirit into the temporal order. In the one Body of Christ, there will always be room for a variety of ministries and for the development of associations, groups, and movements of different types.

As pastors of God's people, we must love legitimate diversity in the Catholic Church and loyally respect and help direct to the common good all authentic charisms wherever they are found among the faithful. It is a part of our own charism to authenticate the discernment of these gifts. The diversity of ministries and institutions allows individuals and communities, under the leadership of the bishops in effective communion with the bishop of Rome, to find their proper way within the universal pilgrimage of the Church.

5. The climate of freedom in the Church should be accompanied by a truly adequate catechesis on ecumenism. Among all the Catholic faithful there should be an open and committed attitude with respect to the ecumenical movement, particularly where there is frequent contact with other Christians. There is a great tradition of pastoral activity in this area on the part of the bishops of the United States. Without treating the subject at length, I would just like to emphasize several related points.

It is necessary to continue to explain the council's teaching that the one Church of Christ "subsists in the Catholic Church" (ibid., 8) and to show how much the Catholic Church desires to see realized within the one Church the unity of all Christ's followers "so that the world may believe" (Jn 17:21).

Any progress that the Catholic Church makes along the path of ecumenism must always be in keeping with the organic development of doctrine. Although the patrimony of faith and moral teaching can be better explained and understood, the essential content of salvation which the Catholic Church has always proclaimed must remain intact. When new doctrinal and moral questions arise, the Church must resolve them with the same principles and with the same logic of faith with which she has acted from her origins under the inspiration of the Holy Spirit.

All the faithful should know the Church's principles governing common worship, or *communicatio in sacris*. These principles were succinctly outlined by the council (cf. *Unitatis Redintegratio*, 8). Their proper application, which has been the constant solicitude of the Holy See, is indeed an effective contribution to authentic ecumenism. Canon 844 is particularly relevant to the question as it concerns the sacraments of penance, the eucharist, and the anointing of the sick. When the reasons regulating the discipline of intercommunion are explained, the eucharistic assembly can more easily understand that there is an indissoluble link between the mystery of the Church and the mystery of the eucharist, between ecclesial and eucharistic communion.

There are many practical opportunities for priests in parishes to explain these principles, such as weddings and funerals. Every effort made to encourage Christians to pray for full Christian unity and to promote it by proper means helps ecumenism. Explaining the conditions for receiving holy communion and the reasons for these conditions fosters the cause of both truth and fraternal love.

6. Much has been done in the United States to bring Christians closer together. The strong desire for full communion has been expressed in ways that amply show the impulse given by the Second Vatican Council, an impulse which the Holy See has constantly upheld in its efforts to implement the council. Catholics have come to acknowledge and esteem the truly Christian endowments from our common heritage which are found among other Christians. An excellent climate has been created for the continuation of a fruitful dialogue between competent experts. Their efforts to find what is held in common and to formulate the controversial points in terms that render them more exact and more intelligible even to those who do not agree upon them are highly commendable.

The Week of Prayer for Christian Unity has continued to emphasize the importance of prayer and other spiritual means to bring about the full communion in faith and charity that is our goal. We are convinced that the union of Christians can only be the fruit of grace, a sign of that forgiveness of God which we must first humbly implore from him.

Prayer in common has greatly strengthened our ties and advanced the cause of true Christian unity. I myself cherish the memory of the service of Christian witness at the University of South Carolina a little more than a year ago.

To be applauded also is the whole network of cooperation among fellow Christians in activities that have a social dimension and that ultimately serve to promote the welfare of all the citizens of your country. I would encourage you, as I also mentioned on my first pastoral visit to the United States, to undertake in common a creative ecumenical action, especially as regards the sacred value of marriage, family life, and the unborn (cf. Ecumenical Prayer Service, October 7, 1979).

In all this, it is essential for us to live a more intense Christian life. The council placed ecumenism in the context of the *"renovatio ecclesiae."* ("renewal of the Church") (*Unitatis Redintegratio,* 6) and saw its immediate source in interior conversion and in holiness of life. This profound conviction continues to be valid.

Special emphasis has to be placed on the dynamic Christocentrism of the ecumenical movement: Union with Christ and love for him is the key to union and love in the Church. From this source, we draw the strength to pursue the evangelizing mission with all its demands.

7. The Church must make herself available to all people. She comes forth from the redeeming love of Christ, who died for all. An important part of this attitude is the Church's respect for different religions. In them, there can frequently be found the *semina verbi,* the presence of a truth that, although hidden in shadow, leads people toward the complete encounter with God in Christ. The Church will always strive to defend these values.

The many "unchurched" people of our cities and towns deserve our special attention and fraternal love. It is necessary that Catholics become closer to them and help them discover their true vocation in Christ. This is the best service we can render to them and the best expression of solidarity and friendship.

Dear Brothers: By God's grace, the Catholic Church in the United States of America has been very fruitful in holiness and love. This has happened in a society that from its origins has been pluralistic and open to all men and women. An important aspect of this vigor of Catholicism is found in the union of truth and freedom. Upon you, pastors of the Church in the United States, rests this great heritage with its immense challenges. I ask Sts. Peter and Paul to support you in your arduous apostolic labors, and I commend you all to Mary, Queen of the Apostles and Mother of Christ's Church.

Ninth Address of His Holiness
Pope John Paul II
to the Bishops of the United States
during Their *Ad Limina* Visits

October 15, 1988

Dear Brothers in our Lord Jesus Christ,

1. It is a special joy for me to welcome all of you, my brother bishops from New York. On this occasion, there comes before my mind so many remembrances of my pastoral visit in 1979. At the same time, I wish to honor in your persons the pilgrimage of faith and love that the millions of Catholic people living in your state are making, in union with Christ, to the Father, in the Holy Spirit.

Today, we are gathered together as pastors, conscious of the words of Jesus to his apostles: "Go, therefore, and make disciples of all nations . . . teaching them to observe all that I have commanded you" (Mt 28:19–20). These words must find a constant echo in our minds and hearts. As successors of the Twelve, we have as our preeminent duty the proclamation of the Gospel to all people (cf. *Christus Dominus*, 12). This is a task that is always necessary, but it is even more urgent wherever there is ignorance, error, or indifference to the truth.

After commanding us to teach, Jesus assures us of his presence and support: "Behold I am with you always, to the end of the age" (Mt 28:20). This promise fills us with peace; it challenges us to confidence and hope. The Lord Jesus Christ sends us forth and remains with us! He wants us to do our part, to carry out our mission, to be vigilant. He wants us ourselves to walk in the light of Christ and to offer this light to the Church and to the world. Today, I wish to refer to a concrete means of offering this light to humanity. It is the Catholic college and university, with its institutional commitment to the word of God as proclaimed by the Catholic Church.

2. As the Second Vatican Council states: "The destiny of society and of the Church herself is intimately linked with the progress of

young people pursuing higher studies" (*Gravissimum Educationis*, 10). Accordingly, the same council exhorts bishops to pay careful pastoral attention to university students. They need this care if they are to sanctify themselves in the exercise of their obligations and "inform culture with the Gospel" (*Sapientia Christiana*, Prologue, 1). The reevangelization of society depends in great part on today's university students. While pursuing their higher studies, they have the right to receive a Catholic formation—both doctrinal and moral— at a level that corresponds to their scholastic endeavors.

The lofty mission of Catholic colleges and universities is to provide a public, enduring, and pervasive influence of the Christian mind in the whole enterprise of advancing higher culture and to equip students to bear the burdens of society and to witness to their faith before the world (cf. *Gravissimum Educationis*, 10). Catholic institutions of higher learning, which educate a large number of young people in the United States of America, have a great importance for the future of society and of the Church in your country. But the degree of their influence depends entirely on preserving their Catholic identity. This Catholic identity has to be present in the fundamental direction given to both teaching and studies. And it must be present in the life of these institutions, which are characterized by a special bond with the Church—a bond that springs from their institutional connection with the Catholic message. The adjective "Catholic" must always be the real expression of a profound reality.

3. We are convinced that it is necessary to respect the legitimate autonomy of human sciences. But we are also convinced that when Christians, with reason enlightened by faith, know the fundamental truths about God, man, and the world, they are in a position to have their intellectual efforts produce more abundant fruits of authentic human progress. Faith does not limit freedom in the pursuit of knowledge. On the contrary, it is its greatest guarantee. This leads us once again to focus our attention on the true significance of freedom in the service of and the search for truth.

"If you remain in my word," Jesus tells us, "you will truly be my disciples, and you will know the truth, and the truth will set you free" (Jn 8:31–32). These words of our Lord proclaim the liberating power of truth. Their profound meaning is easier to grasp when we realize that Christ himself is the truth. It is he, Christ, who contains in himself the complete truth about man; it is he who is the highest revelation of God.

The profound connection between truth and freedom affects the order of all knowledge. In this order, there exists in fact a bond between faith and human knowledge. Truth does not limit freedom. On the contrary, freedom is ordered to truth. Furthermore, the truth of faith does not limit human knowledge. Rather, human knowledge opens up the way that leads to Christian faith, and Christian faith guides human knowledge. While faith does not offer solutions for investigation by reason—which follows its own principles and methodologies in different fields and enjoys a legitimate autonomy—nevertheless, faith assists reason in achieving the full good of the human person and of society.

When Catholic colleges and universities promote true freedom in the intellectual sphere, they provide a singular service for the good of all society. Today's culture, influenced by methods and ways of thinking characteristic of the natural sciences, would be incomplete without the recognition of man's transcendent dimension. Hence, any philosophical current proclaiming the exclusive validity of the principle of "empirical verification" could never do justice to the individual or to society.

The findings of all study can be fully utilized only in consonance with the fundamental truths concerning man—his origin, destiny, and dignity. For this reason, the university by its nature is called to be even more open to the sense of the absolute and the transcendent in order to facilitate the search for truth at the service of humanity.

4. In reflecting on theological knowledge, we turn immediately to faith, since faith is the indispensable foundation and fundamental disposition of all theology. Faith constitutes its starting point and its constant intrinsic point of reference. St. Anselm of Canterbury has given us that well-known definition of the work of theology: "faith seeking understanding." Theology springs from faith, from the desire of the believer to understand the faith.

What faith teaches is not the result of human investigation but comes from divine revelation. Faith has not been transmitted to the human mind as a philosophical invention to be perfected; rather, it has been entrusted to the spouse of Christ as a divine deposit to be faithfully guarded and infallibly interpreted (cf. First Vatican Council: *Dei Filius*, 4; Denzinger Schönmetzer: *Enchiridion Symbolorum*, 3020). In the area of strictly human knowledge, there is room not only for progress toward the truth but also, and not infrequently, for the rectification of substantial error. Revealed truth, however, has been entrusted to the Church once and for all. It has reached its completion in Christ. Hence, the profound significance of the Pauline expression "deposit" of faith (cf. 1 Tm 6:20). At the same time, this deposit allows for a further explanation and for a growing understanding as long as the Church is on this earth.

This task of achieving an ever deeper understanding of the content of faith belongs to every member of the Church. But the Second Vatican Council assures us that "the task of authentically interpreting the word of God, whether written or handed on, has been entrusted exclusively to the living teaching office of the Church" (*Dei Verbum*, 10). This magisterium is not above the divine word but serves it with a specific *carisma veritatis certum* (ibid., 8), which includes the charism of infallibility, present not only in the solemn definitions of the Roman pontiff and of ecumenical councils, but also in the universal ordinary magisterium (*Lumen Gentium*, 25), which can truly be considered as the usual expression of the Church's infallibility.

5. This does not, however, prevent the Church from recognizing and fostering a legitimate pluralism in theology. Right after the council, Paul VI stated that "a moderate diversity of opinions is compatible with the unity of the faith and with fidelity toward the teachings and norms of the magisterium" (*Address to the International Congress on the Theology of the Council,* October 1, 1966). The extent of this pluralism is limited by the unity of faith and the teachings of the Church's authentic magisterium. But within its scope, the plurality of theologies should have a certain conceptual common ground. Not every philosophy is capable of providing that solid and coherent understanding of the human person, of the world, and of God that is necessary to distinguish it clearly from the unity of faith, which depends totally on revealed truth. With respect to the noninfallible expressions of the authentic magisterium of the Church, these should be received with religious submission of mind and will (cf. *Lumen Gentium*, 25).

6. With the passing of time, it is ever more evident how certain positions on the so-called right to dissent have had harmful repercussions on the moral conduct of a number of the faithful. "It has been noted"—I mentioned in my address last year to the bishops gathered in Los Angeles—"that there is a tendency on the part of some Catholics to be selective in their adherence to the Church's moral teachings" (September 16, 1987). Some people appeal to "freedom of conscience" to justify this way of acting. Therefore, it is necessary to clarify that it is not conscience that "freely" establishes what is right and wrong. Using a concise expression of John

Henry Newman's Oxford University sermons, we can say that conscience is "an instrument for detecting moral truth." Conscience detects moral truth: It interprets a norm which it does not create (cf. *Gaudium et Spes*, 16; Paul VI, General Audience, February 12, 1969).

7. Dear Brothers: To carry out the prophetic mission that falls to us as pastors of the Church, it is of great importance to have the collaboration of Catholic theologians and ecclesiastical faculties. As a reflection on the faith, made in faith, theology is an ecclesial science that constantly develops within the Church and is directed to the service of the Church. This is at the root of the theologian's grave responsibility, particularly if he has received the *missio canonica* (cf. *Code of Canon Law*, c. 812) to teach in an ecclesiastical faculty. The authentic faith of theologians nourished by prayer and constantly purified through conversion is a great gift of God to his Church. On it depends the well-being of theology in our day. As I mentioned at The Catholic University in Washington: "It behooves the theologian to be free, but with the freedom that is openness to the truth and the light that comes from faith and from fidelity to the Church" (October 7, 1979).

The Catholic institution in which the bishops of the United States have placed great hope and which they have loyally supported— The Catholic University of America—last year celebrated the 100th anniversary of its founding. Next year will mark the centenary of the granting of its papal charter. All the achievements of the past are due to God's grace, on which is well founded the hope for a future that will see ever greater academic achievements, including those in theological scholarship. In particular, it is to be hoped that this university and all the other Catholic universities and colleges will contribute even more to the enrichment of the Church in the United States and elsewhere, that they will constantly meet their calling to prepare students who are heralds of culture, servants of humanity, and witnesses of faith.

May the Blessed Virgin Mary, *Sedes Sapientiae*, obtain for all of you the light of her son, our Lord Jesus Christ. May she sustain you in pastoral wisdom and bring joy and peace to the hearts of your people.

Tenth Address of His Holiness
Pope John Paul II
to the Bishops of the United States
during Their *Ad Limina* Visits

October 24, 1988

Dear Brothers in our Lord Jesus Christ,

1. My fraternal welcome goes to all of you, the bishops of the ecclesiastical provinces of Cincinnati and Detroit; at the same time, I extend cordial greetings to all the faithful throughout the states of Michigan and Ohio, who are spiritually present here with you today.

The Second Vatican Council reminds us that only Christ has taught the whole truth about man, and he has done so "by the revelation of the Father and his love" (*Gaudium et Spes*, 22). Christ has revealed the greatness of the Father's love not only with words, but above all through the total giving of himself in sacrifice. To see Christ is to see the Father (cf. Jn 14:9). Christ also shows that the Father's love is more powerful than any kind of evil that is in man, in humanity, or in the world (cf. *Dives in Misericordia*, 7). This love is present in the personal history of each human being. To understand the Church of the Incarnate Word, it is necessary to understand God's love.

2. One of the most important expressions of this love is the love of Christian couples. Since "God is love" (1 Jn 4:8), and since man is created in the image and likeness of God, there is inscribed in the humanity of man and woman the "capacity and responsibility of love" (*Familiaris Consortio*, 11). Love in its deepest and richest meaning involves self-giving. Christ, the Son of God and perfect image of the Father (cf. Col. 1:15), gave himself totally in the very fullness of love through his redeeming sacrifice. In the case of husband and wife, genuine love is expressed in the gift of self to each other, which includes giving the power to beget life. In the words of *Gaudium et Spes:* "This love is an eminently human one since it is directed from one person to another through an affection

63

of the will. It involves the good of the whole person. . . . Such love, merging the human with the divine, leads the spouses to a free and mutual gift of themselves" (49). "From one person to another" ("*a persona in personam*"): These few words express a profound truth about conjugal love, a love that is eminently interpersonal. It is a love that involves the gift of the whole person. Included in this gift is their whole sexuality with its openness to the transmission of life.

3. As we commemorate the twentieth anniversary of the teaching of the "prophetic" encyclical *Humanae Vitae* of Paul VI, we see ever more clearly today how relevant and positive it is. In this anniversary year, I wish to make special mention of our pastoral concerns for marriage and family life. I note with interest and gratitude the statement of the National Conference of Catholic Bishops' Committee for Pro-Life Activities commemorating the encyclical. As we all know, marriage is much more than a social institution; it is truly, in Paul VI's words, "the wise institution of the Creator to realize in mankind his design of love" (*Humanae Vitae,* 8). The Church's teaching on marriage is fundamental to understanding the many dimensions of the marriage relationship, especially the sexual dimension. For sexuality is not just a biological reality but concerns the innermost being of the human person as such (cf. *Familiaris Consortio,* 11). It allows spouses to express in a specific way that interpersonal love that binds them together in a permanent, faithful, and exclusive covenant and that leads them to parenthood.

Marriage is a unique type of relationship, and all the actions whereby spouses manifest their love for each other are part of God's plan and signs of his love. In the sexual act, the married couple have the opportunity to grow in grace, in intimacy, in generosity, and in their willingmess to cooperate with God in bringing into being new human persons. But in order to strengthen their love and deepen their unity, married couples must be led to appreciate ever more fully "the inseparable connection, willed by God and unable to be broken by man on his own initiative, between the two meanings of the conjugal act: the unitive meaning and the procreative meaning" (*Humanae Vitae,* 12). In a world that often reduces sex to the pursuit of pleasure, and in some cases to domination, the Church has a special mission to place sex in the context of conjugal love and of generous and responsible openness to parenthood.

4. As pastors, we must encourage couples to maintain an openness to life and a spirit of joyful sharing in regard to children. As

the council has taught us, children are really the supreme gift of marriage and contribute in their own way to making their parents holy (cf. *Gaudium et Spes*, 50, 48). But materialistic and selfish attitudes often deny the value of the child. Each child, however, is a new revelation of God's love and of the fidelity of the spouses. "Each child is also a test of our respect for the mystery of life, upon which, from the very first moment of conception, the Creator places the imprint of his image and likeness" (Christmas Message, 1979).

I deeply appreciate the efforts of your episcopal conference to proclaim the sanctity of human life from conception onward. Throughout the world, we have seen an increase in the number of abortions and a decline in the protection of unborn human life. The bishops of the United States have steadfastly opposed this destruction of human life by programs of education and pastoral care and by advocating laws and public policies that protect and sustain human life, before and after birth. Your annual "Respect Life Program" continues the effort to create respect for human life at every stage and in every circumstance.

This twentieth anniversary of *Humanae Vitae* challenges us once again as pastors to intensify our efforts to present Christian marriage as a vocation to holiness and to help couples understand the role of the Christian family in the life and mission of the Church. We are called to provide engaged and married couples with the fullness of the Church's teaching on human sexuality, conjugal love, and responsible parenthood. We must emphasize the sanctity of human life as a precious gift from God that needs to be protected and fostered, while making greater and more systematic efforts to offer instruction in the natural methods of family planning. Natural family planning enables couples to understand God's design for sex and invites them to dialogue, mutual respect, shared responsibility, and self-control (cf. *Familiaris Consortio*, 32). Our people need to have prayerful confidence that God will bless and sustain them in their efforts to lead lives of holiness and to be witnesses to his love in the modern world.

5. Another indispensable form of witness to God's love for humanity is the practice of the evangelical counsels in consecrated life. The Church profoundly esteems consecrated persons. She rejoices in their consecration and their special witness to love.

Chastity, poverty, and obedience are manifestations of love not only because they are at the root of innumerable and sublime apostolic works which serve the needs of humanity, but above all because they express the power of Christ's paschal mystery, which conquers

65

everything that is opposed to the love of God. To understand love fully, the world needs the sign of the authentic "contradiction" provided by religious consecration. This religious consecration will be authentically actuated in the true love of self-giving when consecrated persons act in union with the Church, in conformity with the teaching and directives of the magisterium of Peter and of the pastors in communion with him (cf. *Redemptionis Donum*, 14–15).

6. The Church offers to the world a witness of singular importance to Christ's love through the celibacy of her priests. Celibacy involves the total gift of self to the Lord for lifelong service in his Church, with the renunciation of marriage for the sake of the kingdom of God. It is a gift that God gives to his Church and that manifests the charity that inspires her. The council showed the courage of faith when it reaffirmed the traditional discipline of celibacy with full confidence that God would not fail to continue to bestow the graces that support this charism.

Priestly celibacy signifies that the priest is not a delegate of the people or even a "functionary" of God, but a true witness to God's love for his people. The rule of celibacy for the Latin Church is more than an ecclesiastical law. It has deep theological and doctrinal roots that confirm its value and show its desirability for those who are chosen to act *in persona Christi capitis* (cf. *Presbyterorum Ordinis*, 2, 6). Last year marked the twentieth anniversary of the encyclical *Sacerdotalis Caelibatus*. May all of us, together with our priests, continue to find inspiration in this teaching as we strive to proclaim the love of Christ in all its fullness.

7. The different forms of witness to God's love for humanity are linked in no small way to the pastoral love of bishops, who teach, govern, and sanctify the people of God. We all know the profound reality to which Jesus himself made reference when he cited the prophetic words: "I will strike the shepherd, and the sheep of the flock will be scattered" (Mt 26:31; cf. Zec 13:7). We should never lose sight of the fact that to a great extent the eternal happiness and even the temporal well-being of innumerable people depend on our own faithfulness to Christ's grace.

Certainly, we face difficulties in exercising our mission as shepherds. Fear may beset our hearts. Will we be understood? Will our message be accepted? How will the world react? How will public opinion judge us? Will our human weakness impede our mission? It is in these moments that we recognize that our love, our pastoral charity, still needs to grow. With St. John we must confess: "Love has no room for fear; rather perfect love casts out all fear. . . . Love

66

is not yet perfect in one who is afraid" (1 Jn 4:18). And because love is a victory over fear, it is a triumph in our ministry.

It is necessary now more than ever to proclaim to the world the truth in love, including "the fullness of truth which sometimes irritates and offends even if it always liberates" (Address of September 5, 1983). In the faithful, persevering, and courageous proclamation of God's word, we pastors must fulfill our mission and our destiny as witnesses of divine love.

The bishop's love for his priests will be a particularly effective expression and sign of the love of Christ. With his deep fraternal and paternal interest in them, with his understanding, human affection, and concern for whatever weighs upon them—while encouraging them to strive for holiness in spite of human weakness—the bishop must help his priests to be witnesses before the people to that love which is at the root of every apostolate. Through the bishop, priests should be able to experience once again the power of Christ's love for all humanity, so that with the beloved disciple they will be able to say: "We have come to know and to believe in the love God has for us" (1 Jn 4:16).

As heralds of Christ's love, we turn to his mother, Mary—*Mater Pulchrae Dilectionis*—to continue in prayer our reflection on that great mystery of love which comes forth from, and returns to, the most Holy Trinity—to whom be glory forever and ever.

Eleventh Address of His Holiness Pope John Paul II to the Bishops of the United States during Their *Ad Limina* Visits

December 9, 1989

Dear Brothers in Jesus Christ,

1. We are coming to the end of the 1988 *ad limina* visits, and I am happy that I can mark this occasion with such a large group of American bishops. To all of you who make up the ecclesiastical provinces of Chicago, Indianapolis, and Milwaukee I extend a welcome of fraternal love.

During this year, I have spoken to your brother bishops on a variety of topics, but always endeavoring to emphasize that the Church in the United States is called to holiness through a life of faith in Jesus Christ, the Son of God and Savior of the world. This emphasis is the consequence of a profound conviction that only through living faith can the Church give a valid pastoral response to all the situations in which she finds herself in the modern world.

In my first talk of the present *ad limina* series, I stressed that the Church in the United States "belongs to Jesus Christ by right. He loves her intensely and intends to possess her more fully and to purify her ever more deeply in every aspect of her ecclesial reality" (March 5, 1988). And today, I would suggest that together we turn our thoughts and hearts once more to Jesus Christ, so that in him we can better understand this ecclesial reality. In the words of the Letter to the Hebrews: "Let us keep our eyes fixed on Jesus, who inspires and perfects our faith" (Heb 12:2). And because "he has taken his seat at the right of the throne of God" (ibid.), it is by looking to Christ in the reality of his heavenly kingdom that we will understand his Church on earth.

2. Since the Church is already the kingdom of God in its initial stage, it is fitting, at the conclusion of the *ad limina* visits, that our attention should be directed to the final consummation of the Church. Her eschatological nature is an essential part of her mystery, and it is of great importance for our pastoral leadership in the Church.

We have been placed by the Holy Spirit as pastors to guide the Church in accomplishing her mission. To do so adequately, we must always keep in mind that there is a specific dynamic at work at the center of the Church's evangelizing activities. It is her eschatological dimension. Everything that brings about her final fulfillment promotes her vitality. But if eschatology were to remain devoid of consequences, the Church's progress would be halted and her course misdirected. In this case, her activities would be irrelevant to authentic evangelization.

Ecclesial communion, too, is profoundly eschatological. Founded on communion through Christ with the Father in the Holy Spirit, the Church knows she is imbued with a life that transcends death. Her life is the life of the risen Christ, the life that through the cross conquered death by the power of loving obedience to the Father's will. By the exercise of his saving power, Christ communicates his own glorious life to the Church. The Church begins to exist as a consequence of this act of the risen Lord. She already lives this life of her Lord and Savior while longing for her definitive fulfillment.

3. By his life-giving act, the Lord brings his Church into union with himself and thus fills her with holiness. But this holiness must be sustained and increased. In all the dimensions of their human existence, the members of the Church must open themselves ever more to the Lord's sanctifying power. In this way, the kingdom gradually takes shape in each Christian and in the Church and grows indefinitely.

It is precisely in holiness that the Church anticipates and actually inaugurates the kingdom of God. The pastoral office in the Church exists to foster holiness. To understand fully the pastoral office, we must look to the holiness of the Church in her eschatological form: the holiness that Christ wills for his Church, the holiness that consummates the union of Christ and his bride in heaven. In presenting an American bishop to the whole world as a model of pastoral charity, Paul VI called the canonization of John Neumann both a "celebration of holiness" and a "prophetic anticipation . . . for the United States . . . of a renewal in love" (June 19, 1977).

The full coming of Christ's kingdom requires from all the faithful the gift of themselves to God and to others. Inseparable from this gift is prayer. We see this in Christ Jesus. Our Lord goes to the cross in the very context of that prayer that he began in Gethsemane and which was consummated when he gave up his spirit into the hands of the Father (cf. Lk 23:46). By virtue of our divine filiation, we are called to follow in this path. Authentic prayer is possible only when we are ready to carry out the saving plan of the Father. We must try, therefore, to help God's people achieve a clear understanding of what prayer means: dialogue with God involving personal commitment. As pastors, we ourselves must bear witness to prayer, being convinced that through it the saving power of God transforms the ecclesial community.

4. The Church proclaims that her members are to be "children of the resurrection" (Lk 20:36), and she waits in joyful hope for the coming of our Savior Jesus Christ. She looks forward to the hour when her glory will be revealed in the fullness of communion with the most Holy Trinity. It is Christ's coming that in turn will definitely inaugurate "new heavens and a new earth" (2 Pt 3:13). As we await these realities, we are called to live in deep peace and serenity. Victory is certain; evil will not prevail: Jesus Christ has overcome the world (cf Jn 16:33).

For this reason, Christians must seek to use temporal goods without the anxiety and hyperactivity of those whose only hope is in this life. Certainly, faith does not permit us to remain passive in the face of suffering and injustice. Our hope spurs us on to work actively for the coming of the universal kingdom of God (cf. *Gaudium et Spes*, 39). But we can never do this with the uncertainty of those who place their ultimate happiness in earthly history. A Christian's struggle breathes serenity and communicates peace, not only as the goal it seeks but as the very style with which it promotes justice. A basic security and optimism inspires the whole life of the Church. We know beforehand the goal to which we aspire with God's help. We may experience hesitation with regard to certain means, but the objective is clear and unchanging. In its light, we can discern the path to be followed, and we correct any course that may have been taken by mistake. The Church can never succumb to the temptation to "remake" herself. Her essential identity is guaranteed by the assurance that Jesus Christ will return in glory.

5. This expectation of Christ's return in glory gives meaning to all the Church's activities and places all temporal concerns in proper perspective. In all she does, the Church looks to a horizon far beyond human history, where everything will be subjected to Christ and by him offered to the Father. At the moment foreordained, everything in heaven and on earth will definitively be placed under the leadership of Christ (cf. 1 Cor 15:24–28). Meanwhile, by God's design, the life of the Church is interwoven in the fabric of human history but always directed to eternal life.

The Church can never be a community at the service of merely temporal objectives. Her end is the kingdom of God, which she must unceasingly extend until its completion in eternity (cf. *Lumen Gentium*, 9). Hence, her initiatives and efforts cannot be motivated by merely temporal values. The Church lives in the midst of human beings—she herself being the new humanity in Christ—and she shares the experience of the whole human family. She lives in solidarity with all people, and nothing human is foreign to her. The concerns of the ecclesial community embrace those of the civil community in such areas as peace, culture, the family, and human rights. Yet, the perspective from which the Church approaches all these issues has as its characteristic originality a relationship with the kingdom of God. If the Church were to lose this transcendent perspective, she could not make her distinctive contribution to humanity.

6. Any consideration of the eschatological dimension of the Church must necessarily include the holy eucharist. The Church constantly finds her nourishment in the sacrament of the Body and Blood of the glorified Christ. At the end of time, the saving power of the eucharist will attain its full effect when the holiness of the Church will be complete and the entire universe will be perfectly restored in Christ. Meanwhile, we "proclaim the death of the Lord until he comes" (1 Cor 11:26).

The renewal of the sacrifice of Christ on Calvary is, at the same time, the banquet of the kingdom. As such, it is the object of the Church's profound solicitude and of her legislation. Recently, there was a clarification of the supplementary character of the faculty granted to lay persons to distribute holy communion as extraordinary eucharistic ministers. The conditions established in the *Code of Canon Law* were authentically interpreted last year, at which time I directed the Congregation for the Sacraments to communicate the decision to the episcopal conferences throughout the world. In some cases, there may still be a need to revise diocesan policies in this matter, not only to ensure the faithful application of the law but also to foster the true notion and genuine character of the participation of the laity in the life and mission of the Church.

As we prepare for the Jubilee of the Year 2000, let us place the sacraments of penance and the eucharist at the center of pastoral renewal. This is in accord with the consistent teaching of the Second Vatican Council, which sees the eucharist as the culmination of the proclamation of the word and the call to penance. The Christ who calls us to the eucharistic banquet is the same merciful Christ who calls us to conversion (cf. *Redemptor Hominis*, 20). It is my earnest hope that in every diocese of the United States, under the pastoral leadership of the bishops, there will be effective plans for the genuine renewal of the sacrament of penance, with the promotion of individual confession. The Church is convinced and proclaims that the implementation of *aggiornamento*, as envisioned by the Second Vatican Council, is closely linked to the renewal of the sacrament of penance. Individual conversion is at the heart of all reform and renewal.

7. Mary, the Mother of Jesus, is the perfect realization of the Church's life of faith and goal of holiness. In her, we have a great sign that sums up and completely expresses the holiness that we sinners strive to attain through conversion. She who is now body and soul in heaven is the first of the redeemed and the totally sanctified one.

In the *Decree on the Apostolate of the Laity*, the council presents a synthesis, applicable to Mary, of living in the temporal order without ever losing sight of the spiritual order in its eschatological fullness. The council says that "while leading the life common to all [here on earth], one filled with family concerns and labors, she was always intimately united with her Son and in an entirely unique way cooperated in the work of the Savior" (*Apostolicam Actuositatem*, 4). In her femininity as virgin, wife, and mother, Mary stands in and before the Church as the woman of all salvation history. Having now been assumed into heaven, she lives her spiritual motherhood interceding on our behalf, helping us in the midst of our earthly pilgrimage not to forget the goal which inspires all the Church's activities.

8. It is our role as bishops to offer to the Father, in union with Christ the High Priest, the Church and all her activities. We offer her as Christ desires her to be: his body and his spouse; the Church of his divinity and his humanity; the Church that reflects his generosity and lives his sacrifice; the Church of truth and merciful love; the Church of prayer and service; the Church of conversion, holiness, and eternal life.

The Church that we offer to the Father and work daily to build up in charity is by no means a so-called monolithic structure, but rather the apostolic structure of unassailable unity, in which, as bishops, all of us are called—in the expression of St. Paul—to "be united in the same mind and in the same purpose" (1 Cor 1:10). Strengthened by this unity, our ministry becomes ever more effective in all its dimensions.

The present hour in the life of the Church calls for great hope, based on the eschatological promises of God and expressed in renewed confidence in the power of Christ's paschal mystery. This is the hour for renewed effort in inviting young people to the priesthood and religious life, the hour for renewed serenity in proclaiming the most difficult demands of Christianity and the loftiest challenges of the cross. It is the hour for a new commitment to holiness on the part of the Church, as she prepares for the great Jubilee of the Year 2000 and invokes the coming of the Lord Jesus.

As we conclude this series of *ad limina* visits, in continuity with those of 1978 and 1983, and with my two pastoral visits to the United States, I wish to renew my deep gratitude to all of you, my brother bishops, for your partnership in the Gospel. In this same spirit, I look forward to the special meeting of bishops planned for next year, so that by continued pastoral collaboration, we may assist the Church in the United States to live her vocation of holiness through a life of dynamic faith. Meanwhile, I entrust to Mary, Mother of the Church and Queen of Heaven, the beloved faithful of your land and bless them all in the name of the Lord Jesus.

Address of His Holiness
Pope John Paul II
to the Byzantine-Ruthenian Bishops
in the United States

Dear Brothers in our Lord Jesus Christ,

1. Through you, I would like to extend warm greetings today to all the Byzantine Catholics of the province of Pittsburgh and, at the same time, to express my love and esteem for all the other Eastern-Rite Catholics in the United States. In your particular churches, there shines forth "that tradition which was handed down from the apostles through the fathers and which forms part of the divinely revealed and undivided heritage of the universal Church" (*Orientalium Ecclesiarum*, 1). Indeed, you bear faithful witness to the catholicity of the Church and to her ability to sustain and develop in the present—in continuity with the past—diverse religious traditions that derive from the one Gospel of our Lord and Savior Jesus Christ.

In your own history, acceptance of the Gospel has exercised a profound influence on your people. The Christian culture that was generated over centuries in your lands of origin and which you have inherited is a great treasure to be preserved, shared, and developed organically in the present situation of your lives in the United States. Acceptance of Christ never fails to produce fruit in all sectors of human activity (cf. *Euntes in Mundum*, 21).

2. The celebration of the recent Marian Year has provided the Church with a special opportunity of appreciating more fully the contribution of the East to the common patrimony of the Church's worship. Here in Rome, on a number of memorable occasions, we have offered the liturgy according to various rites, and in our prayer we have experienced a profound communion with all the Eastern churches. These celebrations vividly expressed the lofty aspirations of the whole Church to adore the majesty of God and to be joined in communion with the most Holy Trinity. The divine plan, according to which the eternal word took on human nature in the womb

75

of the Virgin Mary, continually makes possible the fulfillment of his longing.

Together, we have honored the all-holy Mother of God, the archetype of the human creature's supernatural elevation to union with God in Jesus Christ. Mary, daughter of God the Father, mother of God the Son, spouse and temple of God the Holy Spirit, is at the very heart of the mystery of salvation (cf. *Mulieris Dignitatem*, 3–4). The special place that Marian piety holds in the Eastern churches leads us to a deeper understanding of Christ and, through him, of the Father and the Holy Spirit.

3. From the very beginning of her divine motherhood, Mary takes up her role in relation to the messianic service of Christ, the Son of Man who came not to be served but to serve (cf Mk 10–45), and this service constitutes the foundation of that kingdom in which "to serve" means "to reign." She who is "full of grace" expresses her joy at the gift she has received by saying: "Behold, I am the handmaid of the Lord" (Lk 1:38). As pastors of the Church, we too find joy in our life of service as we recall the challenge of the Second Vatican Council: "In exercising their office of father and pastor, bishops should stand in the midst of their people as those who serve" (*Christus Dominus*, 16). In this our apostolic ministry, we look to Mary as our model of total service.

Among the many tasks incumbent upon bishops, the Second Vatican Council speaks of the obligation "to promote every activity that is of interest to the whole Church, especially that the faith may increase and the light of full truth appear to all people" (ibid.). The service that the laity render in this area is of immense importance and requires a persevering commitment on their part. As they pursue their specific role of consecrating from within all temporal reality, they can be greatly strengthened and inspired by the example of Mary. Thus, in their daily occupations, in their work and family life, they need to be invited to respond to the universal call to holiness by identifying themselves with Christ, by carrying out all their activities as perfectly as possible, and by bearing genuine witness to the Lord and his Gospel. With God's grace, the laity can make their ordinary work a great act of generous and sanctifying service in union with Mary.

The Queen of Apostles is the perfect example of the union of the spiritual and apostolic life in the midst of everyday concerns (cf. *Apostolicam Actuositatem*, 4). She is an incomparable source of inspiration particularly for lay women in today's world which, along with the scientific and technological development that produces material progress for some people and degradation for others, risks becoming steadily more inhuman. The family, the Church, and society need the feminine "genius" which guarantees human sensitivity (cf. *Mulieris Dignitatem*, 30). Through the teaching of the Church, and with the help of the Holy Spirit, women can increasingly discover in Mary the full meaning of their femininity and offer the gift of its untarnished beauty to a world in need of being humanized.

4. Dear Brothers: We are all heirs of a spiritual and civil freedom which has been won at a great price. Many of your people have personally experienced how costly liberty is, especially religious liberty. When we speak about this topic, we are motivated by the truth about man and by concern for the well-being of each nation. Indeed, we have the best interests of all humanity at heart, for religious freedom supports and guarantees all other freedoms. As I said in this year's message for the World Day of Peace, the freedom of individuals and communities to profess and practice their own beliefs is an essential element for peace in the world.

Freedom is hampered in many ways, one of them being the pressures of a secularized cultural environment. You are faithful to your pastoral and prophetic mission when you alert your people, who so prize their religious liberty, not to let the pleasures and allurements of the world deprive them of that inner freedom, which not even persecution itself could destroy in them or their forebears.

5. The presence of Eastern-Rite Catholics in America has come about both as a result of religious persecution in their homelands and through other variously motivated emigrations. Taking their situation into account, the Holy See over the years has fostered the protection and advancement of their ecclesial traditions by establishing parishes and special hierarchies in accordance with their spiritual needs (cf. *Orientalium Ecclesiarum*, 4).

Today, many difficult situations of economic, political, and social unrest have forced millions of people to leave their homes and seek a better life elsewhere. As pastors, we must continually invite the faithful to be sensitive to the needs of the poor and of all who suffer. The "logic of the Gospel" does not permit us to remain passive in regard to anyone in need. The love of Christ impels us, therefore, to defend and support the just cause of migrants, immigrants, and refugees (*Message for World Migrants' Day*, October 4, 1988).

6. By the will of her divine founder, the Church is forever and essentially missionary. On the ecclesial level, your particular churches contribute to the fulfillment of Christ's command to go forth and

make disciples of all nations (cf. Mt 28:19) by displaying to the world the universality of Christ's salvation and by passing on your cherished traditions to successive generations.

Culturally, you bring the heritage of the East to a society that owes much of its formation to Western Christianity. Eastern and Western traditions in Christianity have complemented each other and produced in the fields of music, literature, the visual arts, and architecture, as well as in modes of thought, the inculturation of the one and undivided deposit of faith entrusted by Christ to his Church (cf. *Euntes in Mundum,* 12).

The desire for unity, which is an outstanding sign of our times, is particularly strong at the level of ecumenism. The fathers of the Second Vatican Council expressly thanked God for the communion of the Eastern churches with the See of Peter, the visible foundation of the unity of the Spouse of Christ (*Unitatis Redintegratio,* 17). By helping our Orthodox brethren to reflect on the character of the relations that existed between their churches and the Roman See before separation, your churches contribute greatly to a constructive ecumenical dialogue. Now more than ever, you are called upon to pray and work for building up the visible unity of the Church.

7. Dear Brother Bishops: From your exceedingly rich liturgical and spiritual tradition, with your long experience of faithfulness to Christ in the midst of changes and adversity, you draw the necessary spiritual strength to help the faithful entrusted to your care to correspond to their vocation to holiness and service in the context of the Church in the United States.

As we look forward to the third Christian millenium, let us entrust all our concerns and hopes to the Virgin Mother of God, to whom we owe the birth of Christ and who was present at the birth of the Church, which is one and universal from the beginning. The Marian Year has ended, but the period now opening up before us is a Marian event, a Marian path leading to the year 2000. As we travel this path together, with our eyes raised to her who is indeed the Star of the East, let us constantly present her to our people as a model of service, an incentive to holiness, our Mother of Perpetual Help. Upon you, dear brothers, and upon all the Ruthenian-Byzantine Catholics of the Metropolitan See of Pittsburgh and the eparchies of Passaic, Parma, and Van Nuys—as well as the faithful of all the other Eastern churches in the United States—I invoke the grace and peace of our Lord Jesus Christ, and I impart to all my apostolic blessing.

From the Vatican
November 28, 1988

Joannes Paulus pp. II